ideals®

San Giorgio®-Skinner®
Pasta
Cookbook

Ideals Publishing Corp.
Milwaukee, Wisconsin

Contents

ISBN 0-8249-3019-3

Copyright © MCMLXXXIII by Hershey Foods Corporation.
All rights reserved.
Printed and bound in the United States of America.

Published by Ideals Publishing Corporation
11315 Watertown Plank Road
Milwaukee, Wisconsin 53226
Published simultaneously in Canada.

®The San Giorgio and Skinner Logos are Trademarks of
Hershey Foods Corporation, Ideals Publishing Corporation,
Licensee.

**All recipes were developed and
tested by the San Giorgio-Skinner
Company Kitchens.**

San Giorgio-Skinner Company

A Division of
Hershey Foods Corporation
Hershey, Pennsylvania 17033, U.S.A.

Cover recipe: Fettuccini Carbonara, page 53   *Linguine with Pesto Sauce, page 57*

Pasta Basics

Pasta: A World of Great Nutrition

Call it spaghetti, linguine, rotini, shells, whatever—it's pasta, and it's delicious!

One of our great American favorites, pasta is gaining a reputation as a wonderfully nutritious food as well. And this good-for-you eating is so economical that pasta deserves to be served often—as a star in its own right, as a side dish, or as an "extender" which can help transform other foods into tempting new dishes.

Pasta for Your Health

While there is no ideal diet for everyone because people's needs differ according to age, sex, body size, physical activity, lifestyle, etc., it is generally agreed that complex carbohydrates, the foods generally known as starches, are an essential component of a balanced diet. Carbohydrate is the major and least expensive source of energy for growth and activity. Pasta products are a major source of carbohydrate and also provide other important nutrients.

Why do we need carbohydrates? Basically, carbohydrates are the body's main fuel for growth and activity. Without carbohydrates, the body is forced to use protein or fat for energy. Protein is needed to build and repair tissues and to synthesize hormones and enzymes, so carbohydrates help "save" protein for these important functions.

Carbohydrates are necessary to convert dietary fat to energy. In addition, glucose, a form of carbohydrate, is the primary energy source which can be used by the nervous system and the brain—and it's the main fuel for muscles.

By increasing their consumption of complex carbohydrates, Americans can reduce the amount of animal fat in their diet and add important fiber as well.

Enriched pasta is composed of approximately 74 percent complex carbohydrates. It is low in fat and sodium, and high in valuable nutrients. It contributes 10 percent of the U.S. Recommended Daily Allowance for protein and iron, as well as B vitamins providing 30 percent of the RDA of thiamine and 10 percent of riboflavin and niacin.

Because pasta is often served with other foods—meats, poultry, seafood, cheeses or vegetables—a serving of pasta usually provides additional protein and nutrients as well.

Counting Calories and Pennies

"This is all well and good for people who aren't counting calories," you may say, "but everyone knows that pasta is fattening."

Not so, say nutrition experts. Unfortunately, too many of our notions concerning food are based on inaccurate information and myths.

Five ounces of cooked pasta (two ounces dry weight) contain only 210 calories. A steak of the same weight has more than two times that number of calories. Ounce for ounce, carbohydrates have the same number of calories as protein and half the calories of fat.

Keep in mind, however, that rich sauces and dressings can add unwanted calories. If you are counting calories, avoid cream, oil and butter-based sauces, and use herbs or vegetables.

It's less expensive, too. While many food prices fluctuate by season or region, pasta is almost always a bargain. If you're trying to stretch a budget, a pasta entree is a better buy, both in terms of nutrition and dollars, than an inexpensive cut of meat which may be largely fat. Plan on two to four ounces of dry pasta per person depending on whether it is to be served as a side dish or main course. When cooked, pasta usually doubles in volume.

San Giorgio® **SKINNER®** **Delmonico®** **P&R PROCINO-ROSSI®** **Light 'n Fluffy®**

The five brands that make up the family of San Giorgio-Skinner products are San Giorgio, Skinner, Delmonico, Procino-Rossi and Light 'n Fluffy. These brands are marketed throughout the United States in various geographical locations. San Giorgio-Skinner products are quality enriched pasta made with durum wheat semolina.

Tips on Cooking Pasta

1. Heat three quarts of water* for each one-half pound of pasta, or at least four quarts of water per pound. The more water, the less likely it is that the pasta will stick together. Water should come to a fast boil.

2. Add pasta to the rapidly boiling water gradually, so that the water continues to boil. Cook uncovered, stirring occasionally to keep the pasta from sticking together or sticking to the bottom of the pan, especially during the first minute of cooking time.

3. Do not overcook pasta. Test for doneness by pressing a piece of pasta against the side of the pan with a fork or spoon; pasta will break easily and cleanly when done. Or test by tasting; properly cooked pasta is firm to the bite, or "al dente." If pasta will be baked or cooked further in a recipe, undercook it by about one-third the amount of time given on the package.

4. Drain pasta thoroughly in a large colander. Do not rinse pasta unless it is being used in a salad. Combine with other ingredients, or top with a sauce and serve immediately.

*Add salt for flavor, if desired.

For additional information, contact:
Consumer Information Department
Hershey Foods Corporation
Corporate Administrative Center
14 East Chocolate Avenue
P.O. Box 815
Hershey, Pennsylvania 17033-0815

Pasta Basics

Quality pasta products, such as those from San Giorgio-Skinner, are made from a form of durum wheat known as semolina, which gives them a pale yellow color and a pleasant nutlike flavor. The best pasta holds its shape and texture after cooking.

Most people are familiar with straight spaghetti of famous Italian ancestry, elbow macaroni which knows no particular country of origin but is almost as popular as straight spaghetti, and noodles which tend to be German in background yet are regarded as international and have become an important pasta variety in all American homes. With over 150 different shapes and sizes to choose from, pasta can add almost endless variety to meals. Here's a sample:

Pasta Varieties

1. **FIDEO ENROLLADO**—a curly thin spaghetti broken into small pieces.

2. **FETTUCCINI**—means "small ribbons"; long, thin egg noodles less than half an inch wide; one of the best-known Italian noodles.

3. **RIPPLED EDGE LASAGNE**—very wide, 10-inch long flat pasta with rippled edges, sometimes called Lasagne Noodles. However, lasagne contains no eggs; it merely resembles a noodle shape. Most often used in baked dishes with ricotta and mozzarella cheese and a rich tomato-meat sauce.

4. **RIPPLETS**—narrow, rippled macaroni about 2 inches long; similar to specialty egg noodle products; however, Ripplets contain no eggs.

5. **MACARONI DUMPLINGS**—curled macaroni about 2 inches long; similar to specialty egg noodle products; however, Macaroni Dumplings contain no eggs.

6. **CURLED EGG NOODLES**—tend to be German in background, yet are regarded as international, and have become an important pasta variety in all American homes; come in various thicknesses and widths.

7. **SPINACH NOODLES**—curled egg noodle, ¼ inch wide, containing dried spinach.

8. **LINGUINE**—a member of the spaghetti family; narrow oval rods; a sort of flattened spaghetti.

9. **PERCIATELLI**—"small pierced" pasta; long, hollow like macaroni and about twice the thickness of spaghetti.

10. **SPAGHETTI**—"a length of cord or string" is the metaphor that describes the most famous pasta of all; it is a long solid round rod. Capellini, Vermicelli, Spaghettini, and Spaghetti are all variations in size.

11. **MANICOTTI**—means "small muff"; giant pasta tube, at least 4½ inches long and over an inch in diameter with diagonally cut ends.

12. **SHELL MACARONI**—macaroni shaped like a shell; comes in many sizes, from large for stuffing to tiny for soup.

13. **JUMBO SHELLS**—largest of the shell macaroni family, approximately 4 inches long; an ideal pasta for stuffing.

14. **ROTINI**—means "tiny wheels"; Rotini, Spirals, and Twirls are all the same delightful little twists—with only a change of name.

15. **MOSTACCIOLI**—means "little moustaches"; these medium length tube shapes are also called "ribbed angle cuts" because of their ridged surface and diagonally cut ends.

16. **TWISTED VERMICELLI**—tightly coiled Vermicelli that results from being folded in processing.

17. **CUT ZITI**—a large macaroni; really a tube, about 1⅞ inches long.

18. **TUBETTINI**—tiny tube-shaped pasta.

19. **ACINI DI PEPE**—pasta shaped like peppercorns; great for soups.

20. **RIGATONI**—large, ridged hollow tubes that can be used in casseroles or salads.

21. **ELBOW MACARONI**—small semicircles of hollow tubular pasta; comes in many sizes and lengths.

22. **ORZO**—are about the same size and shape as rice. Orzo are sometimes called "Rosa Marina," which means "rose of the sea."

23. **DITALINI**—small macaroni cut in very short lengths which resemble small thimbles; also called "salad macaroni."

24. **ALPHABETS**—miniature pasta in 26 letter shapes.

25. **RINGS**—small, ring-shaped pasta; offer shape contrast for cubed meats, cheeses, and vegetables, and complement the curves of fruit sections and vegetable slices.

26. **CUT FUSILLI**—also called "curly spaghetti"; adds variety to salads or main dish recipes.

Appetizers

Deviled Pasta

Makes approximately 2 cups.

- ½ cup Tubettini, Alphabets *or* Orzo, uncooked
- 3 hard-cooked eggs, chopped
- ½ cup creamed cottage cheese
- 2 tablespoons prepared mustard
- 2 tablespoons sweet pickle relish *or* chopped pickle
- ¼ teaspoon salt

Cook pasta according to package directions; drain. Rinse with cold water to cool quickly; drain well. Combine remaining ingredients in medium bowl or blender; blend with pastry blender or process in blender until smooth. Stir in cooled pasta; chill. Serve as a dip or use one of the following serving suggestions.

Serving Suggestions

Stuffed Celery: Stuff celery slices; garnish with paprika. Chill.

Filled Pepper Strips: Fill strips of green pepper or sweet red pepper; garnish with paprika or parsley. Chill.

Canapés: Spread on crackers; garnish with black or Spanish olive slice, pimiento strip, parsley sprig or paprika.

Fried Pasta

Makes approximately 4 cups.

- 2 cups Shell Macaroni, Ditalini, Rotini *or* Rigatoni
  Vegetable oil
- ¼ cup grated Parmesan cheese
- ¼ teaspoon garlic salt

Cook pasta according to package directions; drain. Dry on paper towels. Fry pasta, ½ cup at a time, in deep oil in deep-fat fryer or in frypan at 375° for about 2 minutes or until golden brown. Stir to separate. Drain on paper towels. While hot, toss with Parmesan cheese and garlic salt. Cool. Store in airtight container.

Variations

Substitute ¼ teaspoon onion salt for garlic salt.

Omit cheese and sprinkle hot pasta with onion salt or garlic salt.

Fry pasta; do not season. Use as dippers with Guacamole (recipe page 9) or a favorite dip or sauce.

Cheese-Filled Rigatoni

Makes approximately 75.

- 3½ cups (8 ounces) Rigatoni, uncooked
  Vegetable oil
- ¾ cup (8-ounce jar) pasteurized process cheese spread, plain *or* flavored

Fry Rigatoni according to directions for Fried Pasta (recipe this page). When cool, fill both ends with cheese spread.

Shell Appetizers

Makes approximately 65.

- 1¾ cups (4 ounces) Large Shells, uncooked
- ¼ cup Italian salad dressing
- 1 cup (4 ounces) grated Cheddar cheese
- ¼ cup minced dill pickles
- 2 tablespoons Worcestershire sauce
- ⅓ cup chopped almonds
- 15 stuffed green olives, sliced

Cook Large Shells according to package directions; drain. Marinate shells in Italian salad dressing. Blend cheese with pickles, Worcestershire and almonds. Drain shells; fill with cheese mixture. Garnish with olive slices.

Spaghetti Squares

Makes 36.

- 8 ounces Spaghetti, uncooked
- 3 eggs, beaten
- 1 cup sour cream
- 6 tablespoons butter *or* margarine, melted
- ½ cup sliced stuffed green olives
- ¼ cup chopped onion
- ½ teaspoon salt
- ¼ teaspoon paprika
- ¼ teaspoon garlic powder
- ¼ teaspoon white pepper

Cook Spaghetti according to package directions; drain. Combine Spaghetti with remaining ingredients in large mixing bowl. Pour mixture into buttered 9-inch square pan. Set in a pan of hot water; bake at 350° 1 hour. Cut into 1½-inch squares. Fry in fat heated to 375° in deep fryer until golden brown. Drain on paper towels; serve warm. (These squares are also good served hot, but without being fried.)

Note: This recipe can be prepared a day ahead and refrigerated uncut. To serve, cut into squares; allow to reach room temperature before frying.

Shrimp Cocktail Appetizers

Makes approximately 130.

3½ cups (8 ounces) Large Shells, uncooked
1 tablespoon vegetable oil
1 8-ounce package cream cheese, softened
¼ teaspoon lemon juice
½ cup (6-ounce jar) shrimp cocktail
    Dash hot pepper sauce
    Chopped parsley

Cook Large Shells according to package directions; drain. Rinse with cold water to cool quickly; drain well. Toss with oil. Beat cream cheese and lemon juice until smooth. Add shrimp cocktail and hot pepper sauce, beating until well blended. Spoon about 1 teaspoonful of mixture into each shell. Garnish with parsley. Cover with plastic wrap; refrigerate until serving time.

Appetizers Italiano

Makes approximately 130.

3½ cups (8 ounces) Large Shells, uncooked
1 tablespoon vegetable oil
2 8-ounce packages cream cheese, softened
3 to 4 tablespoons milk
½ teaspoon oregano
½ teaspoon minced onion, optional
¼ teaspoon garlic salt
1 4-ounce package sliced pepperoni, chopped

Cook Large Shells according to package directions; drain. Rinse with cold water to cool quickly; drain well. Toss with oil. Beat cream cheese, adding milk gradually, until smooth. Blend in oregano, onion, if desired, and garlic salt; fold in pepperoni. Spoon about 1 teaspoonful of mixture into each shell. Cover with plastic wrap; refrigerate until serving time.

Stuffed Mushrooms

Makes approximately 2 cups filling.

½ cup plus 2 tablespoons (4 ounces) Orzo, uncooked
1 8-ounce package cream cheese, softened
1 egg
2 teaspoons minced onion
    Salt and pepper to taste
    Mushroom caps
    Paprika

Cook Orzo according to package directions; drain. Combine with cream cheese, egg, onion, salt and pepper. Stuff mushroom caps with Orzo mixture; sprinkle with paprika. Bake at 375° 15 minutes or until mushrooms are tender. Serve immediately.

Guacamole

Makes approximately 1 quart.

2 very ripe large avocados, peeled
2 ripe medium tomatoes, peeled, seeded and coarsely chopped
½ cup finely chopped onion
5½ tablespoons (3-ounce can) chopped green chilies, drained
3 tablespoons fresh lime juice
1½ teaspoons salt

Mash avocados with fork to a chunky texture; blend with remaining ingredients. Cover tightly with foil; refrigerate until serving time.

Cream Puff Appetizers

Makes approximately 36.

    Chicken Filling (recipe below)
1 cup water
½ cup butter *or* margarine
1 cup unsifted all-purpose flour
4 eggs

Prepare Chicken Filling. Bring water and butter to a rolling boil in a saucepan. Add flour all at once; stir vigorously over low heat about 1 minute or until mixture leaves side of pan and forms a ball. Remove from heat. Add eggs, one at a time, beating until smooth and velvety. Drop dough by slightly rounded teaspoonfuls onto ungreased baking sheet. Bake at 400° about 25 minutes or until puffed, golden brown and dry. Remove puffs to wire rack; cool slowly away from draft. Just before serving, cut tops off puffs; remove any filaments of soft dough. Fill each puff with Chicken Filling; replace tops.

Chicken Filling

½ cup plus 2 tablespoons (4 ounces) Orzo, uncooked
1½ cups diced cooked chicken
¼ cup finely diced celery
¼ cup finely diced carrot
¼ cup sweet pickle relish
¼ cup mayonnaise
1 tablespoon finely chopped onion
    Salt and pepper to taste

Cook Orzo according to package directions; drain. Rinse with cold water to cool quickly; drain well. Combine with remaining ingredients; refrigerate until ready to fill puffs.

Cheddar-Tuna Quiche

Serves 8.

1¼ cups (8 ounces) Orzo, uncooked
1 egg, slightly beaten
2 tablespoons butter, melted
2 teaspoons chopped parsley
1½ cups (6 ounces) shredded Cheddar cheese
1 6½-ounce can tuna, drained and flaked
1 cup milk
2 eggs
¼ teaspoon salt
¼ teaspoon dry mustard
⅛ teaspoon pepper
6 tomato wedges

Cook Orzo according to package directions; drain. Combine Orzo, beaten egg, butter and parsley. Press mixture firmly against bottom and side of a well-buttered 9-inch pie plate. Sprinkle ¾ cup cheese over crust. Top with half of tuna; sprinkle with remaining cheese. Beat milk, 2 eggs, salt, mustard and pepper; pour over cheese-tuna mixture. Sprinkle remaining tuna on top. Bake, uncovered, at 375° 25 to 30 minutes or until knife inserted near center comes out clean. Arrange tomato wedges on top. Let stand 10 minutes before serving.

Spaghetti Pizza

Serves 8 to 10.

16 ounces Spaghetti, uncooked
2 eggs
½ cup milk
4 cups (16 ounces) shredded mozzarella cheese
½ teaspoon salt
½ teaspoon garlic salt
3½ cups (32-ounce jar) thick spaghetti sauce
1 to 2 teaspoons oregano
½ teaspoon basil
1 4-ounce package sliced pepperoni

Break Spaghetti into 2-inch pieces. Cook according to package directions; drain. Cool. Beat eggs in large bowl; add milk, 1 cup mozzarella cheese, salt and garlic salt. Stir in cooked Spaghetti; mix well. Spread mixture evenly in an oiled 10½ x 15½-inch jelly-roll pan with sides to prevent sauce from running over. Bake at 425° 15 minutes. Remove from oven; reduce temperature to 350°. Spread sauce evenly over Spaghetti; sprinkle with oregano, basil and 3 cups cheese. Top with pepperoni. Return to oven and bake 30 minutes. Let stand 5 minutes before cutting.

Pasta Quiche Lorraine

Serves 8.

Pasta Crust (recipe below)
6 slices bacon, crisply fried, drained and crumbled
1 cup sliced fresh mushrooms
1 cup (4 ounces) shredded Swiss cheese
1 tablespoon finely chopped onion
3 eggs
1½ cups heavy *or* whipping cream
½ teaspoon salt
¼ teaspoon sugar
Dash cayenne

Prepare Pasta Crust. Sprinkle crumbled bacon, mushrooms, cheese and onion in crust. Beat eggs slightly; add remaining ingredients and beat until smooth. Pour into crust. Bake at 425° 15 minutes. Reduce oven temperature to 300°; bake 20 to 30 minutes or until knife inserted 1 inch from center comes out clean. Let stand 10 minutes before cutting.

Pasta Crust

4 ounces Vermicelli *or* Thin Spaghetti, uncooked
2 tablespoons butter
¼ cup grated Parmesan cheese
1 egg, slightly beaten

Cook Vermicelli according to package directions; drain. Toss with butter, Parmesan cheese and egg; press on bottom and up side of a well-buttered 9-inch deep-dish pie plate.

Chicken-Stuffed Shells

Makes approximately 36.

3 cups cooked chicken, cut into thin strips
½ cup soy sauce
1 tablespoon sliced green onion
1 to 2 teaspoons grated onion
1 12-ounce box Jumbo Shells, uncooked
Vegetable oil

Marinate chicken in soy sauce, green onion and onion several hours or overnight. Cook Jumbo Shells according to package directions; drain. Dry on paper towels. Drain chicken. Fill shells with chicken strips; secure with sandwich picks, making sure edges overlap. Fry, a few at a time, in oil in deep-fat fryer or deep frypan at 375° about 2 minutes or until golden brown. Stir to separate. Drain on paper towels. Serve warm.

Soups

Seafood Chowder

Serves 6 to 8.

- ½ cup chopped onion
- ½ cup chopped celery
- 1 clove garlic, minced
- ¼ cup butter *or* margarine
- 1 cup (6½-ounce can) minced clams
- 1 cup (8-ounce can *or* 10-ounce frozen package) oysters
- 1 4¼-ounce can medium shrimp
  Water *or* clam juice
- 5 tablespoons unsifted all-purpose flour
- ⅓ cup dry white wine
- 1 teaspoon chicken base *or* 2 chicken bouillon cubes
- 1 teaspoon salt
- 1 bay leaf
- ½ teaspoon thyme
- ½ teaspoon nutmeg
- ½ teaspoon pepper
- 1 pound frozen *or* fresh codfish fillets, cubed
- ½ cup diced green pepper
- 1⅔ cups (13-ounce can) evaporated milk
- 1 cup milk
- ¼ cup chopped pimiento
- ¼ cup chopped parsley *or* 2 tablespoons dried parsley flakes
- 2½ cups (8 ounces) Shell Macaroni, uncooked

Sauté onion, celery and garlic in butter in 4-quart saucepan until golden. Drain clams, oysters and shrimp, reserving liquids. Combine liquids and add water to measure 3 cups; set aside. Gradually add flour to vegetables in saucepan stirring until well blended. Slowly pour in reserved liquid, stirring constantly until smooth. Add wine, chicken base, salt, bay leaf, thyme, nutmeg and pepper; cover and simmer 15 minutes. Add oysters, codfish and green pepper; simmer 15 minutes uncovered. Remove bay leaf; stir in clams, shrimp, evaporated milk, milk, pimiento and parsley. Heat thoroughly but *do not boil.* Cook Shell Macaroni according to package directions; drain. Stir into chowder.

Noodle Minestrone

Serves 6 to 8.

- ½ cup chopped onion
- 2 tablespoons olive oil
- 2 quarts water
- 1 veal bone
- 1 pound sweet Italian sausage, sliced
- 1½ cups (14-ounce can) red kidney beans, drained
- ½ cup (3-ounce can) chopped mushrooms, undrained
  Salt and pepper to taste
- 1 clove garlic, crushed
- 1 bay leaf
- 1 teaspoon oregano
- 2 cups coarsely chopped zucchini
- 2 cups chopped escarole
- 4 ounces (about 2 cups) Ripplets, uncooked
  Grated Parmesan cheese

Sauté onion in oil in 5-quart saucepan until tender, but not brown. Add water, veal bone, sausage slices, kidney beans, mushrooms, salt, pepper, garlic, bay leaf and oregano. Bring to a boil; reduce heat and simmer, covered, 45 minutes. Remove bone; add zucchini, escarole and Ripplets. Continue to simmer, uncovered, 15 minutes or until Ripplets are tender. Remove bay leaf. Serve with Parmesan cheese.

Minestrone

Serves 6 to 8.

- ½ cup chopped onion
- 1 clove garlic, minced
- 2 tablespoons olive *or* vegetable oil
- 3½ cups (29-ounce can) tomato sauce
- 6 cups water
- 4 cups (20-ounce package) frozen mixed vegetables
- ¼ cup chopped fresh parsley
- 1 teaspoon oregano
- ½ teaspoon basil
- ½ teaspoon salt
  Dash pepper
- 1¼ cups (8 ounces) Tubettini, uncooked

Sauté onion and garlic in oil in 5-quart saucepan until tender, but not brown. Add all ingredients except Tubettini; heat to boiling. Stir in uncooked Tubettini; boil 8 to 10 minutes or until Tubettini is tender.

ABC Meatball Soup

Serves 8.

- 1 cup sliced carrots
- 1 cup diced celery
- ½ cup sliced green onions
- ¼ cup chopped parsley
- 3 beef bouillon cubes
- 3 teaspoons salt
- ½ teaspoon pepper
- 2 quarts water
- 1 egg, slightly beaten
- 2 tablespoons milk
- 1 cup soft bread crumbs
- ¼ cup grated Parmesan cheese
- 1 pound ground beef
- ¾ cup (4 ounces) Alphabets, uncooked
- 1 cup chopped fresh spinach

Combine carrots, celery, onions, parsley, bouillon cubes, 2 teaspoons salt, ¼ teaspoon pepper and water in 5-quart saucepan; bring to a boil. Reduce heat; cover and simmer 20 minutes. Combine egg, milk, remaining 1 teaspoon salt and ¼ teaspoon pepper and bread crumbs; let stand 5 minutes. Add Parmesan cheese and beef; mix well. Shape into 1-inch balls; add to soup and simmer, covered, 15 minutes. Bring to a boil and gradually add Alphabets; simmer, uncovered, about 10 minutes or until Alphabets are tender, stirring occasionally. Remove from heat; stir in spinach.

Noodle Egg-Drop Soup

Serves 4.

- 2 10¾-ounce cans condensed chicken broth
- 1 quart water
- 4 ounces Fine Egg Noodles, uncooked
- 2 eggs, slightly beaten
- 2 tablespoons chopped parsley
- 2 tablespoons butter

Bring chicken broth and water to a boil in 3-quart saucepan. Gradually add noodles, stirring occasionally; cook 8 minutes or until noodles are al dente. Reduce heat to low; stir in eggs and simmer 3 minutes. Remove from heat; stir in parsley and butter.

Old-Fashioned Chicken 'n' Noodles

Serves 8 to 10.

- 1 3-pound frying chicken, cut in serving pieces
- 1 tablespoon salt
- ¼ teaspoon pepper
- 5 cups water
- 1¾ cups sliced celery
- 1½ cups sliced carrots
- ½ cup sliced onion
- 2 tablespoons chopped parsley
- 16 ounces Medium Egg Noodles, uncooked
- ¾ cup (4-ounce can) mushroom stems and pieces, with liquid

Place chicken, salt, pepper and water in 5-quart saucepan or Dutch oven. Bring to a boil; reduce heat and simmer, covered, about 1 hour or until chicken is tender. Remove chicken from broth; cool slightly. Skin and bone chicken; cut into bite-size pieces. Set aside. Measure broth, adding enough hot water to make 6 cups liquid. Return broth to pan; add celery, carrots, onion and parsley. Simmer, covered, about 15 minutes or until vegetables are almost tender. Bring to a boil; stir in Medium Egg Noodles. Boil, uncovered, about 5 minutes or until noodles are tender. Add mushrooms with liquid and chicken; heat to serving temperature.

Ditalini Fagioli

Serves 6 to 8.

- 2 cups (about ½ pound) cubed cooked ham
- ½ cup chopped onion
- 1 clove garlic, minced
- 2 tablespoons butter
- 5 cups water
- 3½ cups (29-ounce can) tomato sauce
- 3 cups (2 15-ounce cans) great northern beans, undrained
- 1 tablespoon chopped parsley
- 1 teaspoon salt
- ¼ teaspoon pepper
- 1¾ cups (8 ounces) Ditalini, uncooked

Sauté ham, onion and garlic in butter in 5-quart saucepan until onion is tender, but not brown. Stir in water, tomato sauce, beans, parsley, salt and pepper; heat to boiling. Reduce heat and simmer 10 minutes to blend flavors. Meanwhile, cook Ditalini according to package directions; drain. Stir Ditalini into soup.

Macaroni with Greek-Style Stew

Serves 6 to 8.

- 2 pounds lean lamb *or* beef, cut in ½-inch cubes
- 2 tablespoons vegetable oil
- 1 cup sliced onions
- 1¾ cups (15-ounce can) tomato sauce
- ¼ cup water
- 1 teaspoon salt
- ½ teaspoon marjoram
- ¼ teaspoon pepper
- 1 small eggplant, cut in ½-inch cubes
- 1 cup diced green pepper
- ½ pound okra, trimmed *or* green beans, cut
- 2 medium tomatoes, peeled and sliced
- 4 cups (16 ounces) Elbow Macaroni, uncooked

Brown meat in oil in 5-quart saucepan; drain off drippings. Add onions; sauté about 5 minutes. Stir in tomato sauce, water, salt, marjoram and pepper. Simmer, covered, 45 minutes. Add eggplant, green pepper and okra. Simmer, covered, 30 minutes or until meat and vegetables are tender. Add tomatoes; cook, uncovered, 5 to 10 minutes, stirring occasionally. Meanwhile, cook Elbow Macaroni according to package directions; drain. Serve stew over macaroni.

Tubettini and Cheese Soup

Serves 6 to 8.

- 1¼ cups (8 ounces) Tubettini, uncooked
- 2 tablespoons chopped onion
- ¼ cup butter *or* margarine
- 3 tablespoons flour
- 2 teaspoons dry mustard
- 1 teaspoon salt
- ¼ teaspoon pepper
- 6 cups milk
- 2 cups (8 ounces) shredded Cheddar cheese
- 2 cups (about ½ pound) cubed cooked ham
- 1¾ cups (10-ounce package) frozen chopped broccoli, thawed and drained

Cook Tubettini according to package directions; drain. Meanwhile, sauté onion in butter in 5-quart saucepan until tender, but not brown. Blend in flour, dry mustard, salt and pepper; cook, stirring constantly, over medium heat for 1 minute. Gradually add milk, stirring until blended. Cook over medium heat, stirring constantly, until mixture thickens. *Do not boil.* Add cheese, ham and broccoli; cook and stir until cheese is melted and broccoli is tender. *Do not boil.* Stir in Tubettini. For a thinner soup, add additional milk.

Chicken and Dumplings

Serves 6 to 8.

- 1 3-pound frying chicken, cut in serving pieces
- 2 cups sliced carrots
- 1 cup sliced celery
- ¾ cup sliced onions
- 2 quarts water
- 6 ounces (about 4 cups) Macaroni Dumplings, uncooked
- Salt and pepper to taste

Place cut-up chicken, carrots, celery, onions and water in 5-quart saucepan or Dutch oven. Bring to a boil; reduce heat and simmer, uncovered, about 1 hour or until chicken is tender. Remove chicken from broth; cool slightly. Skin and bone chicken; cut into bite-size pieces. Set aside. Bring chicken broth to a boil; gradually add Macaroni Dumplings. Boil and stir, uncovered, about 6 minutes or until dumplings are tender. (If you prefer a thicker broth, blend 2 tablespoons flour with ¼ cup water, stir into boiling broth and cook about 1 minute.) Add chicken, salt and pepper to broth; heat to serving temperature.

Grandma's Chicken Fricassee with Noodles

Serves 4 to 6.

- 1 4 to 4½-pound stewing chicken, cut in serving pieces
- 5 cups water *or* enough to barely cover chicken
- 2 teaspoons bouquet garni
- 1½ teaspoons salt
- ⅛ teaspoon pepper
- 8 ounces Wide Egg Noodles, uncooked
- Paprika

Place chicken in 4-quart saucepan or Dutch oven; add water and seasonings. Cover and simmer until chicken is tender. (Allow 2 to 3 hours; time will vary with the bird. Add small quantity of hot water when necessary.) Remove chicken from broth; cool slightly. Skin and bone chicken; cut into bite-size pieces. Set aside. Measure 5 cups of broth; add water if necessary to make 5 cups. Bring to a boil; gradually add Wide Egg Noodles. Boil and stir, uncovered, about 6 minutes or until noodles are tender. Return chicken to noodle mixture; heat thoroughly. Serve sprinkled with paprika.

Soups

P's and Q's Chili Soup

Serves 8 to 10.

    1 cup chopped green pepper
    ½ cup chopped onion
    1 clove garlic, minced
    ¼ cup butter or margarine
    4 cups (40-ounce can) kidney beans with liquid
    3 cups water
    1 10½-ounce can condensed beef broth*
    3 to 4 teaspoons chili powder
    1 teaspoon salt
    ¼ teaspoon pepper
    1 cup (6 ounces) Alphabets, uncooked

Sauté green pepper, onion and garlic in butter in 5-quart saucepan until tender, but not brown. Add remaining ingredients except Alphabets. Bring to boil over medium heat. Reduce heat and simmer 10 minutes to blend flavors. Meanwhile, cook Alphabets according to package directions; drain. Stir Alphabets into soup.

*1½ cups water and 2 beef bouillon cubes may be substituted for condensed beef broth.

Lentil Soup

Serves 6 to 8.

    1¼ cups (½ pound) dried lentils
    2 quarts water
    1 pound leftover ham bone or ham shank*
    1 teaspoon salt
    ½ teaspoon pepper
    1½ cups chopped celery
    1 cup chopped onions
    3 tablespoons vegetable or olive oil
    1¾ cups (8 ounces) Ditalini, uncooked

Soak lentils in about 2 cups water for 5 hours or overnight. Drain and place in 5-quart saucepan. Add 2 quarts water, ham bone, salt and pepper. Cover and simmer 1½ hours. Sauté celery and onions in oil until golden brown; add to soup and simmer, uncovered, 20 minutes. Remove ham bone; dice any remaining meat and add to the soup. Cook Ditalini according to package directions; drain. Stir Ditalini into soup. For a thinner soup, add additional water.

*Recipe can be made with beef soup bone or chicken parts for a flavor variation.

Italian Chicken Soup

Serves 8 to 10.

    1 3 to 4-pound stewing chicken, cut in serving pieces
    4 quarts water
    1½ cups chopped celery
    1½ cups chopped onions
    1 tablespoon chopped fresh parsley
    1 tablespoon salt
    ½ teaspoon basil
    ¼ teaspoon pepper
    4 cups (20-ounce package) frozen mixed vegetables
    2 cups (16-ounce can) tomatoes with liquid, chopped
    1 cup cubed potato (1 medium)
    1¼ cups (8 ounces) Acini di Pepe, uncooked
    Grated Parmesan cheese

Wash chicken; place in 6-quart saucepan with water, celery, onions, parsley, salt, basil and pepper. Bring to a boil; cover and simmer 1½ hours or until chicken is tender. Remove chicken from broth; cool slightly. Skin and bone chicken; cut into bite-size pieces. Add frozen mixed vegetables, tomatoes with liquid and potato; cook, covered, over medium heat 30 minutes or until vegetables are tender. Return chicken to broth. Stir in Acini di Pepe and cook 8 minutes or until pasta is tender. Season to taste; serve hot garnished with grated Parmesan cheese.

Minestrone di Ceci

Serves 6 to 8.

    ¼ pound bacon, diced
    1 cup chopped onions
    2 cloves garlic, minced
    5 cups water
    2 cups (16-ounce can) tomatoes with liquid, cut into small pieces
    1¾ cups (15½-ounce can) chick-peas, drained
    2 cups (10-ounce package) frozen mixed vegetables
    1½ teaspoons basil
    1 bay leaf
    Salt and pepper to taste
    1 cup (6 ounces) Alphabets, uncooked
    Grated Parmesan cheese, optional

Fry bacon in 5-quart saucepan until crisp. Add onions and garlic; sauté until onions are tender, but not brown. Add remaining ingredients except Alphabets and Parmesan cheese; simmer 15 minutes. Stir in uncooked Alphabets; continue to simmer 6 to 8 minutes or until macaroni is tender. Serve Parmesan cheese with soup, if desired.

Spinach Alphabet Soup

Serves 4.

5¾ cups (46-ounce can) chicken broth
1 10-ounce package frozen chopped spinach *or*
½ pound fresh spinach, blanched
1 cup (6 ounces) Alphabets, uncooked
½ pound ham *or* pepperoni, cut into bite-size pieces
1 egg, slightly beaten
2 tablespoons cornstarch dissolved in ¼ cup water
Salt and pepper to taste

Bring broth to a boil in 3-quart saucepan. Add spinach, uncooked Alphabets and ham. Return broth to a boil; cook about 7 minutes or until pasta and spinach are tender. Slowly drizzle egg into broth; do not stir until egg is cooked. Add cornstarch mixture to soup. Cook over low heat until thickened. Season to taste.

Quick and Easy Chicken Soup

Serves 6 to 8.

5¾ cups (46-ounce can) chicken broth
6 cups water
1 cup sliced carrots
1 cup sliced celery
1 cup cubed cooked chicken
½ cup chopped onion
½ teaspoon basil
1 bay leaf
1 cup (6 ounces) Egg Pastina, uncooked
Salt and pepper

Combine chicken broth, water, carrots, celery, chicken, onion, basil and bay leaf in 5-quart saucepan; heat to boiling. Stir in Pastina; boil 4 to 6 minutes or until Pastina is tender. Add salt and pepper to taste.

Beef and Rings Soup

Serves 6 to 8.

1 pound ground beef
1 cup chopped onions
3 quarts water
2 cups (10-ounce package) frozen mixed vegetables
2 tablespoons instant beef bouillon granules
1½ teaspoons salt
¼ teaspoon basil
⅛ teaspoon pepper
1 bay leaf
2¼ cups (8 ounces) Rings, uncooked

Brown ground beef and onions in 6-quart saucepan; drain off excess drippings. Add all ingredients except Rings; heat to boiling. Stir in Rings; boil 8 to 10 minutes or until Rings are tender.

Quick Beef Goulash Stew

Serves 2 to 4.

1 pound ground beef
½ cup chopped onion
1 10¼-ounce can beef gravy
3½ cups (28-ounce can) tomatoes with liquid, chopped
1 cup water
2 tablespoons Worcestershire sauce
1½ cups (10-ounce package) frozen peas and carrots
2 cups Medium Egg Noodles, uncooked
Salt and pepper to taste

Cook ground beef and onion in 3-quart saucepan until meat is browned and onion is tender; drain off excess drippings. Stir in beef gravy, tomatoes with liquid, water and Worcestershire. Bring to a boil; add frozen peas and carrots and uncooked Medium Egg Noodles. Return to a boil. Cover; simmer 10 minutes or until vegetables and noodles are tender. Season with salt and pepper.

Macaroni Gumbo

Serves 8 to 10.

1 cup chopped onions
2 cloves garlic, crushed
¼ cup butter *or* margarine
1 quart water
3½ cups (28-ounce can) tomatoes with liquid, cut into small pieces
2½ cups (2 10-ounce cans) clam broth *or* clam juice
1 tablespoon salt
1 teaspoon oregano
2 bay leaves
¼ teaspoon Tabasco
2½ cups (8 ounces) Shell Macaroni, uncooked
1 10-ounce package frozen cut okra
2 pints shucked oysters, drained
1 pound shrimp, shelled and cleaned
1 6½-ounce can crab meat, drained and boned

Sauté onions and garlic in butter in 5-quart saucepan or Dutch oven until golden. Add water, tomatoes with liquid, clam broth, salt, oregano, bay leaves and Tabasco. Simmer, covered, 40 minutes. Bring to a boil; add Shell Macaroni and okra. Cook, covered, 8 minutes or until macaroni is al dente, stirring occasionally. Stir in oysters, shrimp and crab meat. Cook 5 minutes longer.

Orzo Corn Chowder

Serves 4 to 6.

1¼ cups (8 ounces) Orzo, uncooked
5 slices bacon, diced
½ cup chopped onion
2 cups water
2 cups milk
2 cups (17-ounce can) cream-style corn
1 teaspoon salt

Cook Orzo according to package directions; drain. Meanwhile, fry bacon in 4-quart saucepan until brown. Drain bacon reserving 2 tablespoons drippings; set bacon aside. Return reserved drippings to pan with onion; sauté until onion is tender, but not brown. Add bacon, water, milk, corn and salt; heat to serving temperature. Stir in Orzo.

Manhattan Clam Chowder

Serves 4 to 6.

3 6½-ounce cans minced clams
4 slices bacon
1 cup chopped celery
1 cup chopped onions
2 cups water
1¾ cups (14½-ounce can) tomatoes with liquid, chopped
1 cup (8-ounce can) tomato sauce
½ cup chopped carrots
1 teaspoon salt
½ teaspoon thyme
⅛ teaspoon pepper
1¾ cups (8 ounces) Ditalini, uncooked

Drain clams reserving liquid; set aside. Fry bacon in 4-quart saucepan until crisp. Remove bacon and crumble; set aside. Add celery and onions to bacon drippings; cook until tender, but not brown. Stir in reserved clam liquid, water, tomatoes with liquid, tomato sauce, carrots, salt, thyme and pepper; bring to a boil. Reduce heat; cover and simmer 15 minutes or until vegetables are tender. Cook Ditalini according to package directions; drain. Add Ditalini, clams and crumbled bacon to soup; heat thoroughly. For a thinner soup, add more water or clam juice.

Beef Stew and Dumplings

Serves 6 to 8.

1 pound boneless beef chuck or round, cut into 1-inch cubes
1 tablespoon vegetable oil
2 quarts water
½ cup sliced celery
⅓ cup sliced onion
½ teaspoon salt
⅛ teaspoon pepper
1 bay leaf
1 24-ounce package frozen mixed vegetables
5 beef bouillon cubes
6 ounces (about 4 cups) Macaroni Dumplings, uncooked

Brown beef in oil in 5-quart saucepan. Add water, celery, onion, salt, pepper and bay leaf. Bring to a boil; reduce heat. Simmer, covered, about 1½ hours or until beef is almost tender. Stir in frozen vegetables and bouillon cubes; bring to a boil. Add Macaroni Dumplings and boil, uncovered, about 6 minutes or until dumplings are tender. (If you prefer a thicker broth, blend ¼ cup unsifted all-purpose flour with ¼ cup water and stir gradually into boiling stew. Cook about 1 minute until thickened.)

Macaroni Mushroom Soup

Makes approximately 8 servings.

4 cups (about 1 pound) chopped mushrooms
1 cup chopped carrots
½ cup chopped onion
⅓ cup chopped celery
¼ cup chopped parsley
½ cup butter or margarine
3 cups water
1½ teaspoons salt
¼ teaspoon pepper
⅛ teaspoon nutmeg
1 cup (4 ounces) Ditalini, uncooked
4 cups milk
1 cup light cream
½ cup sherry, optional

Sauté mushrooms, carrots, onion, celery and parsley in butter in 5-quart saucepan until tender, but not brown; add water and seasonings. Bring to a boil. Gradually add Ditalini so that water continues to boil, stirring constantly. Reduce heat; cover tightly and simmer 10 minutes or until Ditalini is tender. Add milk, cream and sherry, if desired; heat to serving temperature.

Salads

Rancho Macaroni Salad

Serves 4 to 6.

2 cups (8 ounces) Elbow Macaroni, uncooked
1½ cups (14-ounce can) red kidney beans, drained
⅓ cup chopped celery
1 cup sour cream
1 cup coarsely chopped sweet mixed pickles
¼ cup sweet pickle juice
2 tablespoons lemon juice
1 teaspoon salt
1 teaspoon dried chives
½ teaspoon onion salt
　 Dash pepper
2 to 3 teaspoons prepared horseradish
½ pound sliced salami, cut into thin strips
　 Crisp salad greens

Cook Elbow Macaroni according to package directions; drain. Rinse with cold water to cool quickly; drain well. Combine macaroni with remaining ingredients except salami and salad greens; toss until all ingredients are evenly coated. Chill. Add salami just before serving; toss. Serve on salad greens.

Best-Ever Shrimp Salad

Serves 6.

2 cups (8 ounces) Elbow Macaroni, uncooked
1 cup diced celery
1½ cups (8-ounce package) frozen tiny shrimp, thawed
1 cup sour cream
¼ cup chili sauce
2 tablespoons prepared horseradish
½ teaspoon dry mustard
½ teaspoon salt
　 Dash marjoram
2 tablespoons minced onion
　 Salad greens
1 medium tomato, cut into wedges

Cook Elbow Macaroni according to package directions; drain. Rinse with cold water to cool quickly; drain well. Combine macaroni, celery and shrimp in large bowl. Combine sour cream, chili sauce, horseradish, mustard, salt, marjoram and onion in small bowl; whip with wire whisk until well blended and of a creamy consistency. Pour dressing over macaroni mixture; toss lightly until blended. Chill. Serve on crisp greens; garnish with tomato wedges.

Macaroni Salad

Serves 4 to 6.

2 cups (8 ounces) Elbow Macaroni, uncooked
1 cup mayonnaise or salad dressing
½ cup finely chopped celery
⅓ cup finely chopped carrot
1 hard-cooked egg, chopped
¼ cup minced onion
2 tablespoons sweet pickle relish
¾ teaspoon dry mustard
¼ teaspoon salt
⅛ teaspoon pepper
　 Dash paprika

Cook Elbow Macaroni according to package directions; drain. Rinse with cold water to cool quickly; drain well. Combine Elbow Macaroni with remaining ingredients; toss lightly. Chill.

Tuna and Elbows

Serves 10 to 12.

4 cups (16 ounces) Elbow Macaroni, uncooked
1 6½-ounce can tuna, drained and flaked
1 cup mayonnaise or salad dressing
1 cup thinly sliced celery
½ cup sliced sweet pickles
1 tablespoon pickle juice
⅓ cup finely chopped onion
⅓ cup chopped carrot
　 Salt and pepper to taste

Cook Elbow Macaroni according to package directions; drain. Rinse with cold water to cool quickly; drain well. Combine Elbow Macaroni with remaining ingredients; toss lightly. Chill.

Creamy Chicken Salad

Serves 4 to 6.

2½ cups (8 ounces) Shell Macaroni, uncooked
3 cups cubed cooked chicken
2 cups sliced carrots
1 cup (8-ounce bottle) creamy cucumber salad dressing

Cook Shell Macaroni according to package directions; drain. Rinse with cold water to cool quickly; drain well. Combine chicken, carrots and Shell Macaroni in large bowl; mix well. Pour salad dressing over macaroni mixture; toss lightly. Chill.

Waldorf Salad

Serves 4 to 6.

1 cup Ditalini, uncooked
1½ teaspoons lemon juice
2½ cups (about 3) unpared, cored and cubed apples
1½ cups seedless grapes
1 cup chopped celery
½ cup mayonnaise
½ cup sour cream
1 cup broken walnuts

Cook Ditalini according to package directions; drain. Rinse with cold water to cool quickly; drain well. Sprinkle lemon juice over apples; toss lightly. Combine with Ditalini, grapes, celery, mayonnaise and sour cream; toss gently. Chill. Sprinkle with walnuts just before serving.

Italian Supper Salad

Serves 4.

1¾ cups (8 ounces) Ditalini, uncooked
¼ pound thinly sliced pepperoni
1 cup thinly sliced zucchini
1 cup coarsely chopped green pepper
½ cup halved black olives
¼ cup chopped fresh parsley
¼ cup chopped pimiento
2 tablespoons sliced green onion
¾ cup olive oil
3 tablespoons wine vinegar
1 clove garlic, minced
1 tablespoon Dijon prepared mustard
½ teaspoon salt
¼ teaspoon pepper

Cook Ditalini according to package directions; drain. Rinse with cold water to cool quickly; drain well. Combine Ditalini, pepperoni, zucchini, green pepper, olives, parsley, pimiento and green onion in large bowl; toss gently. Combine oil, vinegar, garlic, mustard, salt and pepper in screw-top jar or small bowl; shake vigorously or whip with wire whisk until well blended and of a thick and creamy consistency. Pour ⅓ to ½ of dressing over salad; toss gently until ingredients are well coated. Serve remaining dressing with salad or reserve for another salad, if desired.

Goddess Chicken Salad

Serves 8.

2½ cups (8 ounces) Shell Macaroni, uncooked
2 cups cubed cooked chicken
¾ cup thinly sliced celery
⅓ cup thinly sliced radishes
¼ cup chopped pimiento
1 small red onion, sliced and separated into rings
½ teaspoon salt
½ teaspoon pepper
½ cup Green Goddess salad dressing
¼ cup sour cream
6 slices bacon, fried, drained and crumbled

Cook Shell Macaroni according to package directions; drain. Rinse with cold water to cool quickly; drain well. Combine Shell Macaroni with remaining ingredients except bacon. Chill. Before serving, garnish with crumbled bacon.

Macaroni Fruit Salad

Serves 6.

1½ cups (6 ounces) Ditalini, uncooked
1 cup sour cream
1 cup creamed cottage cheese
2 tablespoons chopped pecans
½ teaspoon salt
¼ teaspoon cinnamon
1 cup (11-ounce can) mandarin oranges, drained
2 cups (20-ounce can) pineapple chunks, drained, reserve 3 tablespoons syrup
Salad greens
2½ cups (26-ounce can) apricot halves, drained
Cinnamon, optional
Sour cream, optional

Cook Ditalini according to package directions. Rinse with cold water to cool quickly; drain well. Combine Ditalini, sour cream, cottage cheese, pecans, salt and cinnamon. Add mandarin oranges, pineapple and 3 tablespoons pineapple syrup. Toss lightly; chill. Mound on salad greens; surround with apricots. Sprinkle with cinnamon and serve with additional sour cream, if desired.

Salads

Greek Rotini Salad

Serves 6 to 8.

    3 cups (8 ounces) Rotini, uncooked
    ½ cup olive oil or vegetable oil
    2 tablespoons lemon juice
    ½ teaspoon salt
    ¼ teaspoon pepper
    ¼ teaspoon oregano
    1 clove garlic, crushed
    2 tomatoes, cut into wedges
    1 cucumber, peeled and thinly sliced
    1 cup thinly sliced green pepper strips
    12 black olives or Greek olives
    1½ cups (6 ounces) crumbled Feta cheese
    8 red radishes, thinly sliced
    ¼ cup sliced green onions
    2 tablespoons chopped parsley

Cook Rotini according to package directions; drain. Rinse with cold water to cool quickly; drain well. Combine oil, lemon juice, salt, pepper, oregano and garlic in screw-top jar or small bowl. Shake well or whip with wire whisk until well blended and of a thick and creamy consistency. Chill. Combine Rotini and remaining ingredients in large bowl. Pour dressing over salad; toss gently to coat ingredients evenly. Serve immediately.

Bacon and Tomato Salad

Serves 4 to 6.

    1¼ cups (8 ounces) Tubettini, uncooked
    ⅓ cup mayonnaise
    ⅓ cup vegetable oil
    2 tablespoons wine vinegar
    2 tablespoons catsup
    2 tablespoons grated onion
    ½ teaspoon salt
    ¼ teaspoon pepper
    6 slices bacon, cooked and crumbled
    3 hard-cooked eggs, chopped
    2 tomatoes, cut into wedges

Cook Tubettini according to package directions; drain. Rinse with cold water to cool quickly; drain well. Combine Tubettini and mayonnaise in large bowl. Blend oil, vinegar, catsup, onion, salt and pepper; pour over Tubettini mixture and toss lightly. Chill. Before serving add crumbled bacon and eggs; toss. Garnish with tomato wedges.

Chinese Chicken Salad

Serves 4.

    ⅓ cup soy sauce
    1½ tablespoons sesame or vegetable oil
    1 tablespoon prepared mustard
    2 cups cooked chicken, cut into thin strips
    1¼ cups (8 ounces) Orzo, uncooked
    1 8-ounce package frozen snow peas, cooked, drained and cooled
    ½ cup sliced green onions
    1 cup (8-ounce can) sliced water chestnuts, drained

Blend soy sauce, oil and mustard in medium-size bowl; add chicken and toss lightly until well coated. Allow to stand about 1 hour to blend flavors. Cook Orzo according to package directions; drain. Rinse with cold water to cool quickly; drain well. Gently combine chicken mixture, Orzo and remaining ingredients until blended. Chill.

Taco-Mac Salad

Serves 8 to 10.

    3 cups (8 ounces) Rotini, uncooked
    1 pound ground beef chuck
    1 1½-ounce package taco seasoning
    ½ cup chopped green pepper
    ½ cup minced onion
    1 cup shredded Monterey Jack or Cheddar cheese
    1 pint cherry tomatoes, halved
    ½ head lettuce, shredded
    Salt and pepper to taste
    ¼ cup bottled Catalina French dressing
    1 5½-ounce package taco-flavored corn chips

Cook Rotini according to package directions; drain. Rinse with cold water to cool quickly; drain well. Brown meat in skillet; pour off excess fat. Add taco seasoning and mix well; cool and chill. Combine Rotini, green pepper, onion, cheese, tomatoes, lettuce, salt and pepper in large bowl; mix well. Chill. Just before serving, stir seasoned ground beef and French dressing into salad mixture. Toss lightly. Garnish with corn chips.

Salads

Super Shell Salad

Serves 6 to 8.

- 3½ cups (8 ounces) Large Shells, uncooked
- 1½ cups (10-ounce package) frozen peas, cooked, drained and cooled
- 2 cups sliced raw cauliflower
- 1 cup chopped celery
- 1 cup thinly sliced radishes
- 2 hard-cooked eggs, sliced
- 1 cup mayonnaise or salad dressing
- ½ cup bleu cheese salad dressing
- 2 tablespoons finely chopped green onion
- 1 teaspoon salt

Cook Large Shells according to package directions; drain. Rinse with cold water to cool quickly; drain well. Combine Large Shells, peas, cauliflower, celery, radishes and eggs in large bowl. Combine mayonnaise, bleu cheese dressing, green onion and salt in small bowl; blend well. Pour dressing over macaroni mixture; toss lightly until ingredients are evenly coated. Chill.

Brazilian Salad

Serves 4 to 6.

- 2½ cups (8 ounces) Small Shells, uncooked
- 1 clove garlic
- 2 cups (16-ounce can) peeled tomatoes, drained and cut into small pieces
- 1 cup pitted ripe olives, sliced
- ⅓ cup olive oil
- ⅓ cup chopped fresh parsley
- 1 teaspoon salt
- ¼ teaspoon pepper

Cook Small Shells according to package directions; drain. Rinse with cold water to cool quickly; drain well. Crush garlic in bottom of large bowl. Add Small Shells and remaining ingredients; toss lightly. Chill.

Shell Chicken Salad

Serves 4 to 6.

- 2½ cups (8 ounces) Small Shells, uncooked
- 2 cups diced cooked chicken
- ½ cup diced celery
- ½ cup finely chopped carrots
- ½ cup sweet pickle relish
- ½ cup mayonnaise or salad dressing
- 2 tablespoons chopped onion
- Salt and pepper to taste
- Tomato wedges, optional

Cook Small Shells according to package directions; drain. Rinse with cold water to cool quick-ly; drain well. Combine all ingredients except tomato wedges in large bowl; toss well. Chill. Garnish with tomato wedges, if desired.

Confetti Salad

Serves 6 to 8.

- 2½ cups (8 ounces) Small Shells, uncooked
- ¾ cup bottled Italian salad dressing
- ¾ cup mayonnaise or salad dressing
- 1 teaspoon salt
- ¼ teaspoon pepper
- 4 ounces Cheddar cheese, cubed
- 1 cup chopped raw fresh cauliflower
- ¼ cup finely chopped celery
- ¼ cup finely chopped green pepper
- ¼ cup thinly sliced radishes
- 1 tablespoon chopped parsley

Cook Small Shells according to package directions; drain. Rinse with cold water to cool quickly; drain well. Combine Italian dressing, mayonnaise, salt and pepper in large bowl; blend well. Add all ingredients to the dressing mixture; toss lightly until evenly coated. Chill.

Macaroni-Tomato Surprise

Serves 8.

- 1¾ cups (8 ounces) Ditalini, uncooked
- 2 hard-cooked eggs, chopped
- 1 cup mayonnaise or salad dressing
- 1 tablespoon lemon juice
- ¼ teaspoon celery seed
- ¼ cup chopped green pepper
- ¼ cup chopped green onions
- 8 large tomatoes
- 8 lettuce leaves

Cook Ditalini according to package directions; drain. Rinse with cold water to cool quickly; drain well and toss with eggs. Combine mayonnaise, lemon juice, celery seed, green pepper and green onions; pour over Ditalini and eggs. Mix lightly but thoroughly and chill. Cut tomatoes into wedges, leaving wedges connected at base. Place on lettuce leaves; press tomato sections down to form cups. Fill each with salad mixture.

Macaroni Chicken Salad

Serves 4 to 6.

    2½ cups (8 ounces) Shell Macaroni, uncooked
    ⅓ cup mayonnaise *or* salad dressing
    2 tablespoons lemon juice
    ⅛ teaspoon dry mustard
      Dash Tabasco
    2 cups diced cooked chicken
    1 cup diced celery
    ½ cup chopped sweet gherkins
    2 tablespoons chopped onion
    1 tablespoon chopped pimiento
    1 medium tomato, cut in 8 wedges

Cook Shell Macaroni according to package directions; drain. Rinse with cold water to cool quickly; drain well. Combine mayonnaise, lemon juice, dry mustard and Tabasco in large bowl. Add Shell Macaroni and remaining ingredients except tomato wedges; toss well. Chill. Garnish with tomato wedges.

Tasty Summer Macaroni Salad

Serves 4 to 6.

    2 cups (8 ounces) Elbow Macaroni, uncooked
    1 cup mayonnaise *or* salad dressing
    1 tablespoon vinegar
    1 teaspoon salt
    4 hard-cooked eggs, chopped
    ½ cup sliced radishes
    ½ cup sliced celery
    2 tablespoons sliced green onion
    2 tablespoons chopped parsley

Cook Elbow Macaroni according to package directions; drain. Rinse with cold water to cool quickly; drain well. Combine mayonnaise, vinegar and salt in large bowl; blend well. Add Elbow Macaroni and remaining ingredients; toss lightly until ingredients are evenly coated. Chill.

Italian Garden Salad

Serves 4 to 6.

    1¼ cups (8 ounces) Orzo, uncooked
    1 clove garlic, crushed
    2 cups cherry tomatoes, halved
    2 cups thinly sliced green peppers
    ¼ cup chopped fresh parsley
    1 teaspoon crushed oregano
    1 teaspoon salt
    ½ teaspoon pepper
    ¼ cup grated Parmesan cheese
    ¾ cup bottled Italian salad dressing

Cook Orzo according to package directions. Rinse with cold water to cool quickly; drain well. Combine Orzo with remaining ingredients; toss lightly. Chill.

Hot German Pasta Salad

Serves 4 to 6.

    2½ cups (8 ounces) Shell Macaroni, uncooked
    8 slices bacon
    ½ cup chopped onion
    1 tablespoon flour
    1 tablespoon sugar
    1 teaspoon salt
    ¼ teaspoon celery seed
    ⅛ teaspoon pepper
    ⅓ cup apple cider vinegar
    ¼ cup water

Cook Shell Macaroni according to package directions; drain. While pasta is cooking, fry bacon in skillet until crisp; remove bacon from skillet and drain on paper towels. Cook and stir onion in bacon fat until tender, but not brown. Stir in flour, sugar, salt, celery seed and pepper. Cook over low heat until mixture begins to boil; remove from heat. Stir in vinegar and water. Return to medium heat; cook, stirring constantly, until mixtures comes to a boil. Boil and stir 1 minute; remove from heat. Crumble bacon and add with warm Shell Macaroni to hot dressing. Cook, stirring gently, until shells are coated and heated through. Serve hot.

Ham-Macaroni Salad

Serves 6 to 8.

    2½ cups (8 ounces) Shell Macaroni, uncooked
    ½ cup mayonnaise *or* salad dressing
    2 tablespoons prepared mustard
    2 cups julienne-cut *or* diced cooked ham
    ½ cup chopped onion
    ⅓ cup chopped celery
    ⅓ cup sweet pickle relish
    ½ teaspoon salt
    ¼ teaspoon pepper

Cook Shell Macaroni according to package directions; drain. Rinse with cold water to cool quickly; drain well. Combine mayonnaise and mustard in large bowl. Add Shell Macaroni and remaining ingredients; toss lightly until well blended. Chill.

Pasta Primavera Salad

Serves 4 to 6.

2½ cups (8 ounces) Shell Macaroni, uncooked
2 cups cherry tomatoes, halved
1 cup fresh broccoli flowerets
1 cup thinly sliced zucchini
1 cup sliced fresh mushrooms
½ cup chopped onion
2 tablespoons minced fresh parsley
½ cup bottled Italian salad dressing

Cook Shell Macaroni according to package directions; drain. Rinse with cold water to cool quickly; drain well. Combine with remaining ingredients; toss lightly. Chill.

Spicy Italian Salad

Serves 8.

2 cups (8 ounces) Elbow Macaroni, uncooked
2 large tomatoes, cut into wedges
1 4-ounce package sliced pepperoni, halved
4 ounces Cheddar cheese, cut into ¼-inch cubes
½ cup chopped green pepper
¼ cup chopped celery
2 tablespoons chopped onion
⅔ cup bottled Italian salad dressing
Lettuce leaves
Ripe olive halves

Cook Elbow Macaroni according to package directions; drain. Rinse with cold water to cool quickly; drain well. Combine Elbow Macaroni, tomato wedges, pepperoni, cheese, green pepper, celery, onion and salad dressing; toss lightly. Place in a lettuce-lined bowl; garnish with ripe olives. Cover and chill.

Ditalini Tuna Salad

Serves 6.

1¾ cups (8 ounces) Ditalini, uncooked
1 6½-ounce can tuna, drained and flaked
½ cup mayonnaise or salad dressing
⅓ cup minced onion
⅓ cup sweet pickle relish
¼ cup diced pimiento
1 tablespoon prepared mustard
½ teaspoon salt
¼ teaspoon pepper

Cook Ditalini according to package directions; drain. Rinse with cold water to cool quickly; drain well. Combine Ditalini with remaining ingredients; toss lightly. Chill.

Zippy Mexican Salad

Serves 6 to 8.

2 cups (8 ounces) Elbow Macaroni, uncooked
¾ cup mayonnaise or salad dressing
½ cup chili sauce
2 tablespoons vinegar
2 teaspoons onion salt
1 teaspoon chili powder
4 to 5 drops hot pepper sauce
1½ cups (14-ounce can) red kidney beans, drained
½ cup sliced pitted ripe olives
½ cup minced green onions

Cook Elbow Macaroni according to package directions; drain. Rinse with cold water to cool quickly; drain well. Combine mayonnaise, chili sauce, vinegar, onion salt, chili powder and hot pepper sauce in large bowl; blend well. Add Elbow Macaroni, kidney beans, olives and green onions to the mayonnaise mixture; toss lightly until all ingredients are well coated. Chill.

Gazpacho Salad

Serves 4 to 6.

1 small cucumber, peeled and thinly sliced
2¼ cups (6 ounces) Rotini, uncooked
⅓ cup vegetable oil
5 tablespoons white vinegar
1 clove garlic, crushed
1 teaspoon crushed basil
¼ teaspoon salt
¼ teaspoon pepper
½ pound button mushrooms, cleaned and dried
5 green onions, chopped
2 tablespoons chopped parsley
3 tomatoes, cut into wedges
1 green pepper, seeded and cut into strips

Place cucumber slices in colander; sprinkle some salt on top and allow to drain for 30 minutes. Rinse with cold water; dry thoroughly. Cook Rotini according to package directions. Rinse with cold water to cool quickly; drain well. Combine oil, vinegar, garlic, basil, salt and pepper in large bowl; mix well. Add drained cucumber slices, Rotini, mushrooms, onions and parsley; toss lightly. Chill. Just before serving, add tomato wedges and green pepper strips; toss lightly.

Main Dishes

Vermicelli with Chicken

Serves 4 to 6.

- 1 clove garlic, minced
- ½ cup butter *or* margarine
- 2 cups cubed cooked chicken
- ¾ cup (4-ounce can) sliced mushrooms with liquid
- ¼ cup chopped fresh parsley
- ¼ cup white wine
- ½ cup grated Parmesan cheese
- ⅔ cup milk
  - Dash pepper
- 8 ounces Vermicelli, uncooked

Sauté garlic in 2 tablespoons butter in medium skillet about 1 minute. Add chicken, mushrooms, parsley and wine; cook, stirring constantly, about 3 minutes or until chicken is lightly browned. Set chicken mixture aside in small bowl; keep warm. Melt remaining 6 tablespoons butter in skillet; add cheese, milk and pepper. Cook, stirring constantly, over low heat until cheese melts and sauce is smooth. Meanwhile, cook Vermicelli according to package directions; drain. Gently toss with chicken mixture and cheese sauce until coated.

Shoestring Stroganoff with Shells

Serves 4 to 6.

- 1 pound ground beef
- ½ cup chopped onion
- ½ pound fresh mushrooms, sliced *or* 1½ cups (8-ounce can) sliced mushrooms, drained
- 1 clove garlic, crushed
- 1 10¾-ounce can condensed cream of mushroom soup
- ½ cup water
- 1 teaspoon salt
- ¼ teaspoon pepper
- 1 cup sour cream
- 2½ cups (8 ounces) Shell Macaroni, uncooked

Brown ground beef in large skillet. Add onion, mushrooms and garlic; cook until tender. Stir in soup, water, salt and pepper. Cover; simmer 10 minutes. Just before serving, add sour cream and heat through. *Do not boil.* Cook Shell Macaroni according to package directions; drain. Serve stroganoff over shells.

Macaroni Meat Loaf

Serves 6.

- 2 cups (8 ounces) Elbow Macaroni, uncooked
- ¼ cup butter *or* margarine
- ¼ cup unsifted all-purpose flour
- 1¾ teaspoons salt
- ¼ teaspoon pepper
- 1¼ cups milk
- 1 cup heavy *or* whipping cream
- 3 cups (12 ounces) shredded Cheddar cheese
- 1 egg, slightly beaten
- 1½ cups prepared bread stuffing
- 1½ pounds ground beef

Cook Elbow Macaroni according to package directions; drain. Meanwhile, melt butter in saucepan; blend in flour, ¾ teaspoon salt and ⅛ teaspoon pepper. Gradually add milk and cream. Cook over low heat, stirring constantly, until thickened. Add cheese; stir until melted. Mix macaroni with cheese sauce. Combine egg, stuffing, beef, remaining 1 teaspoon salt and ⅛ teaspoon pepper; spread on bottom of buttered 9 x 13 x 2-inch pan. Cover with macaroni mixture. Bake at 400° 35 minutes or until hot and bubbly.

Fricasseed Chicken with Dumplings

Serves 4.

- 1 3-pound frying chicken, cut in serving pieces
  - Seasoned Flour (recipe below)
- 2 tablespoons vegetable oil
- 2 chicken bouillon cubes dissolved in
  - 1 cup hot water
- ½ teaspoon salt
- ⅛ teaspoon pepper
- ¾ cup (4-ounce can) sliced mushrooms with liquid
- 6 ounces (about 4 cups) Macaroni Dumplings, uncooked

Dredge chicken in Seasoned Flour; brown in oil in 4-quart saucepan. Add bouillon to chicken. Season with salt and pepper; add mushrooms. Cover and simmer 45 minutes or until chicken is tender and sauce is slightly thickened. Cook Macaroni Dumplings according to package directions; drain. Arrange in serving dish; top with chicken and pan gravy.

Seasoned Flour

- ½ cup unsifted all-purpose flour
- 1 teaspoon garlic salt
- 1 teaspoon paprika
- ⅛ teaspoon pepper

Combine all ingredients.

Italian Skillet Dinner

Serves 4 to 6.

- 1 pound ground beef
- 1 cup chopped onions
- 1 cup chopped green pepper
- ½ cup chopped celery
- 1 tablespoon garlic salt
- ½ teaspoon pepper
- 2 cups (16-ounce can) tomatoes with liquid, chopped
- 2 cups (8 ounces) Elbow Macaroni, uncooked
- 2 cups water

Brown ground beef in large skillet. Add onions, green pepper and celery; sauté until tender, but not brown. Add remaining ingredients; stir to blend. Bring mixture to a boil; reduce heat. Simmer, tightly covered, 15 minutes or until macaroni is tender.

Chicken and Noodles in Wine Sauce

Serves 4.

- 1 frying chicken, quartered
  Flour
- ½ cup butter or margarine
- ¼ cup finely chopped onion
- 1 clove garlic, crushed
- ⅛ teaspoon rosemary
- ⅛ teaspoon marjoram
- ¼ cup unsifted all-purpose flour
- 2 cups chicken broth
- 1½ cups small pieces of peeled tomatoes
- 1 teaspoon salt
- ¼ teaspoon pepper
- 1 small bay leaf
- 1 small carrot
- 2 celery ribs
- ½ pound fresh mushrooms, sliced
- ¼ cup white wine
- 8 ounces Wide Egg Noodles, uncooked

Wipe chicken pieces and dredge in flour. Sauté in butter until golden. Remove chicken from pan; set aside. Add onion; sauté until onion is tender, but not brown. Add garlic, rosemary and marjoram; cook a few minutes, but do not brown. Blend in ¼ cup flour. Gradually add chicken broth and cook, stirring constantly, until thickened. Add tomatoes, salt, pepper, chicken, bay leaf, carrot and celery ribs. Simmer 15 minutes. Add mushrooms and wine. Bring to a boil. Cover; reduce heat and simmer 30 minutes or until chicken is tender. Remove bay leaf, carrot and celery. Cook Wide Egg Noodles according to package directions; drain. Arrange chicken pieces over noodles in large serving dish; top with sauce.

Spaghetti and Chicken

Serves 6 to 8.

- ½ pound mushrooms, sliced
- 10 tablespoons butter or margarine
- ½ cup unsifted all-purpose flour
- 1¾ cups (13¾- or 14½-ounce can) chicken broth
- 1½ cups milk
- 1½ cups diced cooked chicken
  Salt and pepper to taste
- 16 ounces Spaghetti, uncooked
- ½ cup grated Parmesan cheese

Sauté mushrooms in butter in 3-quart saucepan. Blend in flour; gradually stir in chicken broth and milk. Cook over low heat, stirring often, until sauce thickens; add chicken, salt and pepper. Cook Spaghetti according to package directions; drain. Add cheese to sauce and heat; *do not boil.* Toss Spaghetti with sauce.

Lasagne

Serves 10 to 12.

- 1 pound ground beef
- 3½ cups (32-ounce jar) spaghetti sauce
- 1 pound Rippled Edge Lasagne, uncooked
- 4 cups (2 pounds) ricotta cheese
- 2 cups (8 ounces) shredded mozzarella cheese
- ¼ cup grated Parmesan cheese
- 4 eggs
- 1 tablespoon parsley
- 1 teaspoon salt
- ¼ teaspoon pepper
  Grated Parmesan cheese, optional

Brown meat in 3-quart saucepan; add sauce and simmer 10 minutes. Cook Lasagne according to package directions for about 10 minutes; drain well. Separate Lasagne and lay flat on waxed paper or aluminum foil to keep pieces from sticking together. Combine cheeses, eggs, parsley, salt and pepper for filling. Pour about ½ cup sauce on bottom of 9 x 13 x 2-inch pan. Arrange 4 pieces of Lasagne lengthwise over sauce, overlapping the edges. Spread ⅓ cheese filling over Lasagne and cover with about 1 cup meat sauce. Repeat layers of Lasagne, cheese and meat sauce twice. Top with a layer of Lasagne and remaining meat sauce; sprinkle with additional Parmesan cheese, if desired. Cover with aluminum foil; bake at 350° about 30 minutes or until hot and bubbly. Remove foil; bake about 10 minutes until lightly browned. Allow to stand about 10 minutes before cutting.

Pork with Capellini

Serves 4.

4 pork chops *or* sausage patties (4 ounces each)
1¾ cups (15½-ounce jar) spaghetti sauce
½ cup water
1 tablespoon instant minced onion
1½ teaspoons oregano
¾ teaspoon basil
½ teaspoon garlic salt
⅛ teaspoon cayenne
8 ounces Capellini, uncooked
  Grated Parmesan *or* Provolone cheese, optional

Brown pork chops in skillet; drain off fat. Combine sauce, water, onion, oregano, basil, garlic salt and cayenne; stir into meat. Cover and simmer, stirring occasionally, 30 minutes for pork chops or 20 minutes for sausage patties. Remove cover and cook a few minutes longer if thicker sauce is desired. Cook Capellini according to package directions; drain. Serve Capellini with hot sauce and meat. Garnish with grated cheese, if desired.

Family Goulash

Serves 4.

1 pound lean ground beef
½ cup sliced onion
1 small clove garlic, minced
1 cup water
½ cup catsup
1 tablespoon Worcestershire sauce
2 teaspoons brown sugar
2 teaspoons paprika
1 teaspoon salt
½ teaspoon dry mustard
  Dash pepper
1 tablespoon cornstarch *or* flour blended with
  2 tablespoons water
6 ounces Egg Noodles, uncooked

Brown ground beef in large skillet. Add onion and garlic; cook and stir until onion is tender. Combine 1 cup water, catsup, Worcestershire, brown sugar, paprika, salt, mustard and pepper; stir into ground meat mixture. Cover; simmer 15 minutes. Add cornstarch and water to meat mixture. Cook and stir 5 minutes or until sauce thickens and begins to boil. Cook Egg Noodles according to package directions; drain. Serve goulash over noodles.

Mostaccioli Medley

Serves 4.

1½ cups thinly sliced carrots
1 cup thinly sliced celery
⅓ cup chopped onion
1 clove garlic, minced
2 tablespoons olive *or* vegetable oil
2 to 3 cups cubed cooked turkey *or* ham
1¾ cups (14½-ounce can) tomatoes with liquid, cut
  into small pieces
1¾ cups (15-ounce can) tomato sauce
1 cup dry white wine *or* apple juice
¼ cup chopped parsley
½ teaspoon basil
½ teaspoon salt
¼ teaspoon pepper
3 cups (8 ounces) Mostaccioli, uncooked

Sauté carrots, celery, onion and garlic in oil until tender, but not brown. Stir in remaining ingredients except Mostaccioli. Simmer, uncovered, 20 minutes to blend flavors. Meanwhile, cook Mostaccioli according to package directions; drain. Toss with hot sauce.

Quick Fry Pork 'n' Noodles

Serves 4.

¼ cup unsifted all-purpose flour
1 teaspoon salt
¼ teaspoon pepper
1½ pounds lean loin pork chops, boned and cut into
  ¼-inch strips
1 8-ounce can pineapple chunks in pineapple juice
3 tablespoons white vinegar
2 tablespoons soy sauce
1 tablespoon cornstarch
1 tablespoon sugar
2 tablespoons vegetable oil
2 green peppers, halved, seeded and cut into strips
½ cup chopped onion
6 ounces Wide Egg Noodles, uncooked

Combine flour, salt and pepper in plastic bag; shake pork strips in bag to coat well. Drain pineapple reserving juice. Add water to pineapple juice to equal ¾ cup. Combine juice, vinegar, soy sauce, cornstarch and sugar; reserve. Fry pork strips in hot oil in skillet about 5 minutes or until browned. Stir in green pepper, onion and reserved pineapple juice mixture; cover and simmer 5 minutes. Cook Wide Egg Noodles according to package directions; drain. Stir pineapple chunks into pork mixture; heat thoroughly. Serve over noodles.

Main Dishes

Spaghetti with Veal and Peppers

Serves 6 to 8.

  2 pounds boneless veal shoulder, cut in strips
    Flour
  ⅓ cup olive or vegetable oil
  ¼ cup butter or margarine
  4 medium green peppers, cut in strips
  ½ cup sliced onion
  4 cloves garlic, minced
3½ cups (28-ounce can) tomatoes with liquid
  2 cups (2 8-ounce cans) tomato sauce
1½ teaspoons salt
1½ teaspoons basil
  ¼ to ½ teaspoon oregano
  ⅛ teaspoon pepper
 16 ounces Spaghetti, uncooked

Dredge veal in flour; brown in oil and butter in large skillet. Remove meat; sauté green peppers and onion about 5 minutes. Add meat, garlic, tomatoes with liquid, tomato sauce and seasonings. Cover and simmer 1 hour, stirring occasionally. Cook Spaghetti according to package directions; drain. Serve with veal sauce.

Oriental Shrimp Toss

Serves 4.

  1 cup (8-ounce can) sliced water chestnuts
    with liquid
  2 tablespoons butter
  ¼ cup soy sauce
  ¼ teaspoon dry mustard
  ¼ teaspoon garlic powder
  ¼ teaspoon pepper
  3 cups shredded cabbage
  2 cups (2 8-ounce cans) sliced bamboo shoots,
    drained
  ½ cup chopped celery
  ¼ cup chopped green pepper
  ¼ cup chopped onion
  1 6-ounce package frozen cooked tiny shrimp,
    thawed
  1 10¾-ounce can condensed cream of
    shrimp soup
  3 cups (8 ounces) Rotini, uncooked

Drain water chestnuts reserving liquid; set aside. Melt butter in 10-inch skillet. Add reserved water chestnut liquid, soy sauce, dry mustard, garlic powder and pepper; bring to a boil. Add drained water chestnuts, cabbage, bamboo shoots, celery, green pepper, onion and shrimp. Stir-fry until vegetables are tender-crisp. Stir in soup; heat through. Meanwhile, cook Rotini according to package directions; drain. Toss with shrimp and vegetable sauce.

Macaroni Oriental

Serves 12.

  2 pounds thinly sliced beef sirloin or boned loin of
    pork, cut in strips
  ⅓ cup butter or margarine
  ½ pound fresh mushrooms, sliced
  4 cups diagonally sliced celery
  1 cup sliced onions
  1 cup green onion slices
  1 cup (8-ounce can) sliced bamboo shoots, drained
  4 beef bouillon cubes dissolved in 2 cups hot water
  ¼ cup cornstarch
  ½ cup soy sauce
  4 cups (16 ounces) Elbow Macaroni, uncooked
    Soy sauce, optional

Sauté meat in butter in 5-quart saucepan or Dutch oven until lightly browned (if using pork, sauté 5 minutes); add mushrooms and sauté 2 minutes. Add celery, onions, green onions, bamboo shoots and bouillon; cook, covered, 3 minutes. Blend cornstarch with soy sauce. Stir into meat and vegetable mixture; boil 1 minute. Cook Elbow Macaroni according to package directions; drain. Arrange meat and vegetable mixture over macaroni. Serve with additional soy sauce, if desired.

Spaghetti Royale

Serves 4.

  ¼ cup butter or margarine
  ¼ pound mushrooms, sliced
  1 cup green pepper strips
  ½ cup chopped onion
  1 tablespoon chopped parsley
  ½ teaspoon thyme
  ¼ cup unsifted all-purpose flour
1½ teaspoons salt
2½ cups chicken stock
  2 cups diced cooked chicken
  1 4-ounce jar pimientos, drained and diced
  1 tablespoon lemon juice
  8 ounces Spaghetti, uncooked

Melt butter in saucepan. Add mushrooms, green pepper, onion, parsley and thyme; cook until vegetables are tender. Blend in flour and salt. Gradually add chicken stock; cook, stirring constantly, until thickened and boiling. Add chicken, pimientos and lemon juice. Stir and heat to serving temperature. Cook Spaghetti according to package directions; drain. Toss with chicken mixture.

Italian-Style Short Ribs

Serves 4.

    3 pounds short ribs, cut into 2-inch pieces
      Seasoned Flour (recipe page 28)
    2 tablespoons vegetable oil
    1 cup chopped celery
    ½ cup chopped onion
    1 clove garlic, minced
    1 cup beer *or* water
    1¾ cups (14½-ounce can) tomatoes with liquid,
      chopped
    1½ teaspoons salt
    1 teaspoon Italian seasoning
    ¼ teaspoon lemon and pepper seasoning
    ¼ teaspoon basil
    8 ounces Medium Egg Noodles, uncooked
    1 tablespoon butter
    1 tablespoon chopped parsley

Dredge short ribs in Seasoned Flour. Brown well in oil in Dutch oven. Remove ribs and drain, reserving 2 tablespoons fat. Add celery, onion and garlic to reserved fat; sauté 2 minutes. Add beer and stir to scrape meat particles loose. Add tomatoes with liquid, salt and seasonings. Return ribs to pan; cover and simmer 1½ hours or until ribs are tender. Cook Medium Egg Noodles according to package directions; drain. Toss with butter and parsley. Serve with short ribs and gravy.

Note: For a thicker gravy, blend 2 tablespoons flour into ¼ cup water; stir into gravy. Cook, stirring constantly, about 3 minutes or until hot and slightly thickened.

Veal Cutlet-Macaroni Dinner

Serves 4.

    ½ cup chopped onion
    1 clove garlic, chopped
    1½ teaspoons butter
    4 boned veal cutlets (3 ounces each)
    1 cup tomato purée
    1¾ cups (14½-ounce can) tomatoes with liquid,
      chopped
    1 teaspoon salt
    1 teaspoon oregano
      Dash pepper
    1 cup (4 ounces) Elbow Macaroni, uncooked
      Snipped parsley

Sauté onion and garlic in butter until onion is tender, but not brown. Add veal cutlets; brown on both sides. Stir in tomato purée, tomatoes with liquid, salt, oregano and pepper. Cook, stirring occasionally, over low heat until veal is

tender, about 30 minutes. Meanwhile, cook Elbow Macaroni according to package directions; drain. Arrange on serving platter. Top with veal cutlets, sauce and parsley.

Noodles with Flounder Roll-Ups

Serves 4 to 6.

    2 pounds flounder fillets
      Seasoned salt
    1 cup bread crumbs
    ½ cup grated Cheddar cheese
    2 tablespoons chopped parsley
    ¼ cup butter *or* margarine, melted
    2 tablespoons lemon juice
    6 ounces Medium Egg Noodles, uncooked
      Chopped parsley

Sprinkle flounder with seasoned salt. Combine bread cubes, cheese and parsley; place some on center of each fillet. Roll up and secure with sandwich picks. Place in buttered shallow baking dish. Drizzle with butter and lemon juice. Bake at 350° 25 minutes or until fish flakes when tested with a fork. Cook Medium Egg Noodles according to package directions; drain. Place on serving plate; sprinkle with parsley. Arrange flounder roll-ups on noodles and top with pan juices.

Party Macaroni Chili

Serves 10.

    2 pounds ground beef round
    3 tablespoons olive *or* vegetable oil
    3½ cups (28-ounce can) tomatoes with liquid,
      chopped
    1 quart tomato juice
    2 cups chopped onions
    3 cloves garlic, minced
    4 teaspoons salt
    2 tablespoons chili powder
    ½ teaspoon ground cumin
    ½ teaspoon oregano
    ½ teaspoon Tabasco
    1 bay leaf
    1½ cups (14-ounce can) red kidney beans, drained
    1 cup chopped sweet mixed pickles
    2 cups (8 ounces) Elbow Macaroni, uncooked

Brown beef in oil in 5-quart saucepan or Dutch oven. Add tomatoes with liquid, tomato juice, onions, garlic, salt and remaining seasonings. Simmer, covered, 1 hour; stir in kidney beans and pickles. Cook 30 minutes longer. Remove bay leaf. Cook Elbow Macaroni according to package directions; drain. Combine with chili.

Main Dishes

Meat-Filled Jumbo Shells
Serves 10 to 12.

- 1 12-ounce box Jumbo Shells, uncooked
- 1 pound ground beef
- 1 pound ground pork
- 4 eggs, slightly beaten
- 1 cup flavored bread crumbs
- 1 cup (4 ounces) shredded mozzarella cheese, optional
- ¾ cup finely chopped onions
- ¾ teaspoon oregano
- ½ teaspoon salt
- ⅛ teaspoon pepper
- 3½ cups (32-ounce jar) spaghetti sauce
  Grated Parmesan cheese, optional

Cook Jumbo Shells according to package directions; drain well. Cool in a single layer on waxed paper or aluminum foil to keep shells from sticking together. Brown beef and pork in skillet; drain. Combine meat, eggs, bread crumbs, mozzarella cheese (if desired), onions, oregano, salt and pepper. Fill each shell with about 2 tablespoons meat mixture. Spread a thin layer of sauce on bottom of 9 x 13 x 2-inch baking pan. Place shells, open side down, in single layer in pan; cover with remaining sauce. Sprinkle with Parmesan cheese, if desired. Cover with aluminum foil; bake at 350° 45 minutes or until hot and bubbly.

Chicken Cacciatore
Serves 6.

- 4 slices bacon, diced
- ⅓ cup chopped onion
- 1 clove garlic, minced
- ¾ cup (4-ounce can) sliced mushrooms, drained
- 3½ cups (32-ounce jar) spaghetti sauce
- 1 teaspoon salt
- 1 teaspoon oregano
- ¼ teaspoon pepper
- 1 2½- to 3-pound frying chicken, cut up or 2 cups cooked chicken strips
- ½ cup vegetable oil
- 16 ounces Linguine, uncooked

Sauté bacon in large saucepan until tender. Add onion, garlic and mushrooms; cook until onion is tender. Stir in sauce, salt, oregano and pepper; simmer about 10 minutes. Sauté chicken in oil in large skillet until browned on all sides. Add chicken to sauce; cover and simmer 45 minutes for chicken pieces or 20 minutes for chicken strips or until chicken is tender. Cook Linguine according to package directions; drain. Arrange chicken over Linguine in large serving dish.

Chicken Vegetable Sauté
Serves 4 to 6.

- 1 clove garlic, minced
- 1 cup thinly sliced zucchini
- 1 cup thinly sliced fresh mushrooms
- ½ cup thinly sliced onion
- 2 tablespoons vegetable oil
- 1¾ cups (14½-ounce can) tomatoes with liquid, chopped
- 1 cup cubed cooked chicken or turkey
- ½ cup water
- 1 teaspoon basil
- ½ teaspoon salt
- ⅛ teaspoon pepper
- 3 cups (8 ounces) Rotini, uncooked

Sauté garlic, zucchini, mushrooms and onion in oil until tender, but not brown. Add remaining ingredients except Rotini; simmer 15 minutes. Cook Rotini according to package directions; drain. Serve chicken and vegetables over Rotini.

Barbecued Ribs with Spaghetti
Serves 4 to 6.

- 4 pounds pork spareribs
- 1 onion, stuck with cloves
- 1 celery rib
- 1 carrot
- 2 cups (2 8-ounce cans) tomato sauce
- 1½ cups water
- ¼ cup light brown sugar
- ¼ cup Worcestershire sauce
- ¼ cup lemon juice
- 2 teaspoons salt
  Dash Tabasco
- 1 onion, cut in thin slices
- 1 lemon, cut in thin slices
- 8 ounces Thin Spaghetti, uncooked

Cut ribs into 4-rib portions. Place in large pot; cover with salted water. Add onion with cloves, celery and carrot. Bring to a boil; reduce heat and simmer, covered, 45 minutes. Meanwhile, combine tomato sauce, water, brown sugar, Worcestershire, lemon juice, salt and Tabasco in saucepan. Bring to a boil; reduce heat and simmer 30 minutes. Drain ribs; pat dry with absorbent paper. Place ribs, meaty side up, in a roasting pan; place onion and lemon slices over ribs. Bake at 325° about 1 hour or until tender, basting frequently with tomato sauce. If sauce becomes too thick, add more water. Cook Thin Spaghetti according to package directions; drain. Mix with 1 cup of tomato sauce. Arrange on serving platter; place ribs on top of spaghetti. Serve with remaining sauce.

Chicken Cacciatore (top)
Chicken Vegetable Sauté (middle)
Meat-Filled Jumbo Shells (bottom)

Main Dishes

Skillet Stroganoff

Serves 4 to 6.

- 1 pound ground beef
- 1 clove garlic, minced
- 1 tablespoon vegetable oil
- 1 envelope (½ of 2¾-ounce box) dry onion soup mix
- ½ teaspoon ginger
- ¼ teaspoon pepper
- 6 ounces (about 4 cups) Ripplets, uncooked
- ¾ cup (4-ounce can) sliced mushrooms, undrained
- 3 cups hot water
- 2 tablespoons flour
- 1 cup sour cream

Brown ground beef and garlic in oil in 10-inch skillet. Sprinkle soup mix, ginger and pepper evenly over meat. Arrange uncooked Ripplets evenly in layer over meat. Add mushrooms with liquid; pour hot water over Ripplets, making sure all are moistened. Cover tightly. Cook over medium heat until pan is steaming; reduce heat to low and simmer, covered, 8 minutes or until Ripplets are tender. Blend flour into sour cream; stir into stroganoff. Cook about 3 minutes longer or until slightly thickened.

Pork Tenderloin with Noodles

Serves 4 to 6.

- 1½ pounds pork tenderloin, cut in 1-inch slices and flattened
  Salt and pepper
  Flour
- 3 tablespoons vegetable oil
- 2 tablespoons chopped onion
- 2 tablespoons chopped celery
- ¾ cup (4-ounce can) sliced mushrooms with liquid
- 1¼ cups chicken broth
- 1 tablespoon Worcestershire sauce
- 8 ounces Medium Egg Noodles, uncooked

Sprinkle pork tenderloin lightly with salt and pepper, then dredge in flour. Fry slowly in oil in skillet until meat is browned; remove meat and sauté onion and celery. Stir in mushrooms with liquid and chicken broth. Add browned pork; cover and simmer over low heat until meat is tender, about 1 hour. Stir in Worcestershire; simmer, uncovered, about 10 minutes. Cook Medium Egg Noodles according to package directions; drain. Place pork tenderloin on platter; surround with noodles. Top with gravy.

German Elbows

Serves 4.

- 6 slices bacon
- 1 pound frankfurters or knockwurst, sliced diagonally in 1-inch pieces
- 4 cups shredded cabbage (about ¾ pound)
- 1 cup sliced onions
- ½ cup water
- ⅓ cup cider vinegar
- 2 tablespoons sugar
- 1 teaspoon salt
- ¼ teaspoon pepper
- 2 cups (8 ounces) Elbow Macaroni, uncooked
- 1 tablespoon caraway seed, optional

Fry bacon in large skillet until crisp; drain, reserving drippings. Crumble bacon; set aside. Add frankfurters, cabbage, onions, water, vinegar, sugar, salt and pepper to bacon drippings. Cover; cook over low heat 10 to 15 minutes or until cabbage is tender, stirring occasionally. Cook Elbow Macaroni according to package directions; drain. Toss with cabbage mixture, crumbled bacon and caraway seed, if desired.

Mostaccioli with Mushrooms and Peas

Serves 4 to 6.

- ¼ pound bacon
- ½ pound fresh mushrooms, sliced
- ¼ cup chopped onion
- 1 clove garlic, minced
- 2 cups (16-ounce can) tomatoes with liquid, chopped
- 2 cups (10-ounce package) frozen peas, thawed and drained
- 6 fresh basil leaves or 1 tablespoon dried basil
- ½ teaspoon salt
- 3 cups (8 ounces) Mostaccioli, uncooked

Fry bacon in large skillet until crisp; drain, reserving drippings. Crumble bacon; set aside. Sauté mushrooms, onion and garlic in bacon drippings until tender, but not brown. Add tomatoes with liquid, peas, basil and salt; bring to boil over medium heat. Reduce heat; simmer 20 minutes, stirring occasionally. Cook Mostaccioli according to package directions; drain. Toss with tomato mixture and bacon.

Macaroni and Short Ribs

Serves 4.

   2 pounds beef short ribs
   1 tablespoon vegetable oil
1½ cups water
   ⅓ cup catsup
   1 teaspoon salt
   ⅛ teaspoon pepper
   1 teaspoon oregano
   2 carrots, cut in ½-inch slices
   1 turnip, peeled and diced
   ½ cup chopped onion
   2 cups (8 ounces) Elbow Macaroni, uncooked
      Paprika

Cut short ribs into serving pieces. Brown in oil in large skillet over medium heat. Add water, catsup, salt, pepper and oregano. Cover, lower heat and simmer 1 hour. Add vegetables; continue simmering 1 hour. Cook Elbow Macaroni according to package directions; drain. Arrange macaroni on large platter, heaping high in center. Place short ribs at either end; top with sauce. Sprinkle with paprika.

Spinach Lasagne

Serves 10 to 12.

   1 pound Italian sausage, casing removed
   ½ cup chopped onion
3½ cups (32-ounce jar) spaghetti sauce
   ½ cup water
   ¼ cup red wine or 2 teaspoons sugar
   2 teaspoons parsley flakes
2½ teaspoons salt
   1 teaspoon oregano
   ½ teaspoon pepper
   1 pound Rippled Edge Lasagne, uncooked
   2 cups (15-ounce container) ricotta cheese
   4 eggs
1¼ cups (10-ounce package) frozen chopped spinach, cooked and drained
   2 cups (8 ounces) shredded mozzarella cheese
   ½ cup grated Parmesan cheese

Sauté sausage in pan until evenly browned. Drain all but 2 tablespoons fat from pan; add onion and sauté until lightly browned. Add sauce, water, wine, parsley, 1½ teaspoons salt, ¾ teaspoon oregano and ¼ teaspoon pepper; simmer 15 to 20 minutes. Cook Lasagne according to package directions for about 10 minutes; drain. Separate and lay flat on waxed paper or aluminum foil to keep pieces from sticking together. Combine ricotta, eggs, 1 teaspoon salt, ¼ teaspoon pepper, ¼ teaspoon oregano and

spinach. Pour about ½ cup sauce on bottom of 9 x 13 x 2-inch pan. Arrange 4 pieces of Lasagne lengthwise over sauce, overlapping the edges. Spread ⅓ of cheese-spinach mixture over Lasagne; sprinkle with ½ cup mozzarella and 2 tablespoons Parmesan. Cover with about 1 cup sauce. Repeat layers of Lasagne, cheese-spinach mixture, mozzarella, Parmesan and sauce twice. Top with a layer of Lasagne and remaining sauce; sprinkle with remaining ½ cup mozzarella and 2 tablespoons Parmesan. Cover with foil; bake at 375° 40 to 45 minutes. Allow to stand about 10 minutes before cutting.

Old-Fashioned Pot Roast

Serves 6 to 8.

   1 4-pound eye of round or beef rump roast
   2 tablespoons vegetable oil
   ¼ pound mushrooms, sliced
   1 cup sliced onions
   1 large carrot, halved
   1 celery rib, halved
   2 cloves garlic, minced
1¼ teaspoons salt
   2 beef bouillon cubes
   ¼ teaspoon pepper
   2 bay leaves
   ⅔ cup (6-ounce can) tomato paste
   1 cup plus 3 tablespoons water
   2 tablespoons flour
   2 tablespoons chopped parsley, optional
  16 ounces Wide Egg Noodles, uncooked

Brown meat on all sides in oil in Dutch oven. Remove meat and drain off fat. Combine vegetables, garlic, salt, bouillon cubes, pepper, bay leaves, tomato paste and 1 cup water in pan; heat to boiling. Return roast; cover and simmer 2½ hours or until meat is tender. Discard carrot, celery and bay leaves. Remove meat to platter; keep warm. Blend flour into 3 tablespoons water; stir into cooking liquid. Cook, stirring constantly, until gravy boils. Boil and stir 1 minute; stir in parsley, if desired. Cook Wide Egg Noodles according to package directions; drain. Toss with small amount of gravy. Serve with pot roast and remaining gravy.

Casseroles

Elbows and Chicken Casserole

Serves 4.

  2 cups (8 ounces) Elbow Macaroni, uncooked
  ¼ cup chopped onion
  ¼ cup butter *or* margarine
  1 10¾-ounce can condensed cream of celery soup
  1 cup milk
  2 cups cubed cooked chicken
1½ cups (10-ounce package) frozen peas and carrots, thawed and drained
  ¼ cup flavored bread crumbs
  2 tablespoons melted butter *or* margarine
  ½ teaspoon poultry seasoning

Cook Elbow Macaroni according to package directions; drain. Sauté onion in ¼ cup butter in 2-quart saucepan until tender, but not brown. Add soup and milk; stir until smooth. Stir in chicken, peas and carrots and macaroni; place in buttered 2-quart casserole. Combine bread crumbs, 2 tablespoons melted butter and poultry seasoning; sprinkle on top of macaroni mixture. Bake, uncovered, at 375° 20 to 25 minutes or until hot and bubbly.

Ham, Rotini and Broccoli Casserole

Serves 6.

  1 pound fresh broccoli, cut into 1-inch pieces
  ¼ cup butter *or* margarine
  6 tablespoons unsifted all-purpose flour
  1 teaspoon onion powder
  ½ teaspoon salt
  ¼ teaspoon white pepper
  ¼ teaspoon dry mustard
  4 cups milk
  2 cups (8 ounces) shredded Cheddar cheese
  3 cups (8 ounces) Rotini, uncooked
  ½ pound cooked ham, cut into ½-inch cubes
  ¼ cup grated Parmesan cheese

Cook broccoli in boiling salted water until slightly underdone; drain. Melt butter in 2-quart saucepan; blend in flour, onion powder, salt, pepper and mustard. Gradually add milk; cook, stirring constantly, until thickened. Add Cheddar cheese; stir until cheese is melted and sauce is smooth. Meanwhile, cook Rotini according to package directions; drain. Combine broccoli, Rotini, ham and cheese sauce until well blended. Place in buttered 3-quart casserole; sprinkle with Parmesan cheese. Bake, uncovered, at 375° 20 minutes or until hot and bubbly.

Baked Ziti and Cheese

Serves 4 to 6.

  ½ pound sweet Italian sausage
  1 cup sliced mushrooms
  1 cup 2-inch green pepper strips
  ⅓ cup chopped onion
  ½ cup butter *or* margarine
  ⅓ cup unsifted all-purpose flour
2¼ cups milk
  2 cups (8 ounces) shredded Cheddar cheese
  ½ cup grated Parmesan *or* Romano cheese
  ½ teaspoon salt
  ½ teaspoon pepper
  3 cups (8 ounces) Cut Ziti, uncooked

Bake sausage at 350° 30 minutes; cool. Slice sausage in thin pieces; set aside. Meanwhile, sauté mushrooms, green pepper and onion in butter in 4-quart saucepan until tender, but not brown; remove vegetables from pan and set aside. Blend flour into butter in saucepan; gradually stir in milk. Cook, stirring constantly, over medium-low heat until mixture begins to boil; boil and stir 1 minute. Add 1½ cups Cheddar cheese, Parmesan cheese, salt and pepper; stir until cheeses are melted and mixture is smooth. Set aside and keep warm. Cook Ziti according to package directions; drain. Stir sausage slices, sautéed vegetables and Ziti into cheese sauce. Pour mixture into buttered 2-quart casserole or baking dish. Sprinkle with remaining ½ cup Cheddar cheese. Cover with foil; bake at 350° 20 minutes. Remove foil; bake about 10 to 15 minutes longer or until top is browned.

Baked Tuna and Dumplings

Serves 4.

  6 ounces (about 4 cups) Macaroni Dumplings, uncooked
  1 10¾-ounce can condensed cream of mushroom soup
1¼ cups milk
  ⅓ cup grated Parmesan *or* Romano cheese
  ¼ cup chopped pimiento *or* stuffed olives
  1 6½-ounce can tuna, drained and flaked
    Dash pepper

Cook Macaroni Dumplings according to package directions; drain. Combine soup, milk, cheese, pimiento, tuna and pepper in buttered 2-quart casserole; fold in dumplings. Bake, uncovered, at 350° 15 to 20 minutes or until bubbly and lightly browned.

Casseroles

Baked Ziti and Eggplant

Serves 4 to 6.

- ½ pound sweet Italian sausage, casing removed
- 1 clove garlic, minced
- 2 cups (½ pound) eggplant, pared and cut into julienne strips
- ¾ cup sliced fresh mushrooms
- ⅓ cup chopped onion
- ¼ teaspoon salt
  Dash pepper
- 3 cups (8 ounces) Cut Ziti, uncooked
- 3½ cups (32-ounce jar) spaghetti sauce
- 1 cup (4 ounces) shredded mozzarella cheese
- ¼ cup grated Parmesan cheese

Brown sausage in skillet; add garlic, eggplant, mushrooms and onion. Sauté until vegetables are tender and lightly browned; drain off excess fat. Add salt and pepper; set aside. Cook Ziti according to package directions; drain. Combine Ziti with 2 cups sauce. Spread ¼ cup sauce on bottom of 9-inch square baking dish. Arrange half of Ziti in pan; spoon eggplant mixture evenly over Ziti and top with ½ cup sauce, ⅔ cup mozzarella and 2 tablespoons Parmesan. Cover with remaining Ziti, sauce and cheeses. Bake at 350° 25 minutes.

Chinese-Style Chicken and Noodles

Serves 6.

- 6 ounces Wide Egg Noodles, uncooked
- 2 cups diced cooked chicken
- ½ pound fresh mushrooms, sliced
- 3 tablespoons butter
- 2 tablespoons cornstarch
- 2 tablespoons green pepper flakes
- 2 tablespoons chicken-seasoned stock base
- 3 cups hot water
- ¼ cup soy sauce
- 1 cup (8-ounce can) sliced water chestnuts, drained
- 2 tablespoons instant minced onion
- ½ cup slivered toasted almonds

Cook Wide Egg Noodles according to package directions; drain. Combine with chicken in 3-quart casserole. Sauté mushrooms in butter until tender. Stir in cornstarch, green pepper flakes, chicken stock base and water; cook, stirring constantly, until sauce begins to boil. Stir in soy sauce, water chestnuts and onion. Pour over noodles and chicken; mix well. Sprinkle with almonds. Bake, covered, at 350° 20 to 30 minutes or until hot and bubbly.

Italian Shell Bake

Serves 6 to 8.

- 2½ cups (8 ounces) Shell Macaroni, uncooked
- 1 pound ground beef
- 1 cup chopped onions
- 1 cup chopped green pepper
- 1¾ cups (15-ounce can) tomato sauce
- 1 teaspoon garlic salt
- 1 teaspoon oregano
- ¼ teaspoon pepper
- 2 cups (15-ounce container) ricotta cheese
- 2 cups (8 ounces) shredded mozzarella cheese
- ¼ cup chopped fresh parsley

Cook Shell Macaroni according to package directions; drain. Meanwhile, brown ground beef in large skillet. Add onions and green pepper; sauté until tender, but not brown. Pour off excess fat. Stir in tomato sauce, garlic salt, oregano and pepper; simmer 5 minutes. Combine ricotta, 1½ cups mozzarella and parsley; mix well. Combine shells with meat sauce; place ½ of mixture into 2½-quart casserole. Spread cheese filling evenly over shells; top with remaining shells and meat sauce mixture. Sprinkle with remaining ½ cup mozzarella. Cover; bake at 350° 25 minutes. Remove cover; bake 5 minutes longer or until cheese is lightly browned.

Baked Shells and Sausage

Serves 4 to 6.

- 1 pound sweet Italian sausage
- ½ cup chopped onion
- 1 clove garlic, minced
- 3½ cups (8 ounces) Large Shells, uncooked
- 1 cup ricotta cheese
- 3½ cups (32-ounce jar) spaghetti sauce
- 2 cups (8 ounces) shredded mozzarella cheese
- 3 tablespoons grated Parmesan cheese

Sauté sausage in skillet until well browned on all sides. Remove from pan; slice into thin pieces. Return to pan and add onion and garlic; sauté until onion is tender, but not brown. Cook Large Shells according to package directions; drain. Combine shells, sausage mixture and ricotta; mix well. Pour ½ cup sauce on bottom of 3-quart casserole. Spread ⅓ of shells and sausage mixture over sauce; cover with 1 cup sauce. Sprinkle ¾ cup mozzarella and 1 tablespoon Parmesan over sauce. Repeat layers of shells and sausage mixture, sauce, mozzarella and Parmesan cheese twice, ending with Parmesan cheese. Cover; bake at 400° 20 to 30 minutes or until hot and bubbly.

Rotini Provolone

Serves 4 to 6.

- ½ cup chopped onion
- 2 tablespoons butter
- 1 pound ground beef
- 2 cups (2 8-ounce cans) tomato sauce
- ¾ cup (4-ounce can) sliced mushrooms, drained
- 1 teaspoon salt
- ½ teaspoon garlic salt
- ½ teaspoon oregano
- ⅛ teaspoon pepper
- 3 cups (8 ounces) Rotini, uncooked
- 2 cups (8 ounces) shredded Cheddar cheese
- ¾ cup (3 ounces) shredded Provolone cheese

Sauté onion in butter until tender, but not brown. Add beef and cook until meat is brown. Mix in tomato sauce, mushrooms, salt, garlic salt, oregano and pepper; simmer 15 minutes. Meanwhile, cook Rotini according to package directions; drain. Toss with meat sauce. Place ⅓ of mixture in 2-quart casserole; top with ⅔ cup Cheddar and ¼ cup Provolone. Repeat layers of Rotini mixture, Cheddar and Provolone cheeses twice. Bake, uncovered, at 375° 20 to 25 minutes or until hot and bubbly.

Macaroni Casserole Italiano

Serves 4.

- 1 envelope (1½ ounces) spaghetti sauce mix with mushrooms
- ⅔ cup (6-ounce can) tomato paste
- 2 cups water
- ½ pound hot Italian sausage, parboiled 4 minutes and sliced
- ½ pound ground beef
- ½ cup chopped onion
- ½ teaspoon salt
- 2 cups (8 ounces) Elbow Macaroni, uncooked
  Grated Parmesan cheese

Blend sauce mix, tomato paste and water in 2-quart saucepan; set aside. Brown sausage slices in skillet; add to sauce. Brown beef with onion and salt in sausage drippings, stirring frequently. Stir into sauce and bring to a boil. Simmer, covered, 25 to 30 minutes. Meanwhile, cook Elbow Macaroni according to package directions; drain. Combine with meat sauce in 2-quart casserole; sprinkle cheese on top. Bake, uncovered, at 375° 20 minutes or until hot and bubbly.

Baked Tuna and Shells

Serves 4 to 6.

- ¼ cup chopped onion
- ¼ cup butter or margarine
- ¼ cup unsifted all-purpose flour
- 3 cups milk
- 1 cup (4 ounces) shredded sharp cheese
- 1 teaspoon salt
  Dash each pepper and nutmeg
- 1 6½-ounce can tuna, drained and flaked
- ¼ cup chopped fresh parsley
- 2 tablespoons chopped pimiento
- 3½ cups (8 ounces) Large Shells, uncooked

Sauté onion in butter until tender, but not brown; blend in flour. Gradually add milk. Cook, stirring constantly, over medium heat until mixture begins to boil; boil and stir 1 minute. Remove from heat. Add cheese, salt, pepper and nutmeg; blend well until cheese is melted. Stir in tuna, parsley and pimiento; keep warm over low heat. Cook Large Shells according to package directions; drain. Toss with warm sauce mixture; turn into buttered 2-quart casserole. Cover; bake at 350° 25 minutes.

Cheese 'n' Spinach Noodle Casserole

Serves 4 to 6.

- 1¼ cups (10-ounce package) frozen chopped spinach
- 2 cups (1 pound) cottage cheese
- 2 cups (8 ounces) shredded Cheddar cheese
- 3 eggs
- 1 teaspoon garlic salt
- 12 ounces Wide Egg Noodles, uncooked
- 3½ cups (32-ounce jar) spaghetti sauce

Cook spinach according to package directions for 1 minute; drain. Press out excess moisture. Combine spinach, cottage cheese, Cheddar cheese, eggs and garlic salt; set aside. Cook Wide Egg Noodles according to package directions; drain. Combine with 2½ cups sauce. Arrange half the noodles in bottom of 3-quart casserole. Spread the spinach mixture evenly over noodles; cover with remaining noodles. Spread remaining sauce over top. Cover and bake at 350° 30 to 35 minutes or until hot and bubbly.

Cheese and Shell Bake

Serves 6 to 8.

   1 pound ground beef
   ½ cup chopped onion
   ½ cup chopped green pepper
   1¾ cups (15-ounce can) tomato sauce
   1 teaspoon garlic salt
   ¼ teaspoon pepper
   1½ cups (6 ounces) shredded Cheddar cheese
   1 cup sour cream
   1 tablespoon chopped fresh parsley
   5 cups (16 ounces) Small Shells, uncooked

Brown ground beef in skillet. Add onion and green pepper; sauté until tender, but not brown. Pour off excess fat. Stir in tomato sauce, garlic salt and pepper; simmer 5 minutes. Combine 1 cup cheese, sour cream and parsley; mix well. Cook Small Shells according to package directions; drain. Pour 1 cup meat sauce in bottom of 3-quart casserole; stir in half the shells. Spread cheese filling evenly over the shells. Top with remaining shells and meat sauce. Sprinkle with remaining ½ cup shredded cheese. Cover; bake at 350° 20 minutes. Remove cover; bake about 5 minutes longer or until cheese is lightly browned.

Shells and Vegetable Casserole

Serves 4.

   2½ cups (8 ounces) Small Shells, uncooked
   ¼ cup butter or margarine
   ¼ cup unsifted all-purpose flour
   ½ teaspoon salt
   ⅛ teaspoon pepper
   2 cups milk
   2 cups (8 ounces) shredded Cheddar cheese
   2 cups (10-ounce package) frozen mixed vegetables, cooked and drained

Cook Small Shells according to package directions; drain. Melt butter in medium saucepan; blend in flour, salt and pepper. Cook over medium heat, stirring constantly, until mixture boils. Boil and stir 1 minute; gradually add milk, stirring constantly until mixture thickens. Add 1½ cups cheese; stir until cheese is melted and mixture is smooth. Combine cheese sauce, mixed vegetables and Small Shells in bowl; place in buttered 2-quart casserole. Sprinkle remaining ½ cup cheese on top; cover and bake at 350° 20 minutes. Remove cover; bake about 5 minutes longer or until cheese is melted and lightly browned.

Chicken Tetrazzini

Serves 4.

   3 cups (8 ounces) Rotini, uncooked
   ¼ cup butter or margarine
   ¼ cup unsifted all-purpose flour
   1 cup chicken broth
   1 cup heavy or whipping cream
   ½ cup shredded Gruyère or Swiss cheese
     Dash white pepper
   2½ to 3 cups diced cooked chicken
   ¾ cup (4-ounce can) sliced mushrooms, drained
   ½ teaspoon salt
   ⅓ cup grated Parmesan cheese

Cook Rotini according to package directions; drain. Melt butter in large saucepan; blend in flour. Gradually stir in broth and cream. Cook, stirring constantly, over low heat until sauce thickens. Mix in shredded cheese and pepper; heat and stir until cheese melts. Remove from heat; stir in chicken, mushrooms and salt. Add Rotini to sauce; toss lightly. Place in buttered 2-quart casserole. Sprinkle with Parmesan cheese. Broil 5 to 7 minutes or until lightly browned.

Swiss Noodle Bake

Serves 6 to 8.

   12 ounces Egg Noodles, uncooked
   1½ cups (10-ounce package) frozen peas, thawed and drained
   ¾ cup (4-ounce can) sliced mushrooms, drained
   ¼ cup sliced green onions
   ½ cup butter or margarine
   ⅓ cup unsifted all-purpose flour
   1 teaspoon salt
   ½ teaspoon white pepper
   3 cups milk
   2 cups (8 ounces) shredded Swiss cheese
   2 cups cubed cooked ham
   1 cup (16-ounce can) tomatoes, chopped and well drained

Cook Egg Noodles according to package directions; drain. Sauté peas, mushrooms and onions in 2 tablespoons butter in small saucepan 3 minutes; remove from heat and set aside. Melt remaining 6 tablespoons butter in medium saucepan; remove from heat. Add flour, salt and white pepper; stir until smooth. Return to heat; gradually add milk, stirring constantly until thickened. Add cheese; stir until smooth and thick. Combine Egg Noodles, sautéed vegetables, cheese sauce, ham cubes and tomatoes; blend well. Place in buttered 3-quart casserole. Cover; bake at 350° 25 to 30 minutes or until hot and bubbly.

Casseroles

Broccoli-Noodle Casserole

Serves 4.

- 6 ounces Extra Wide Egg Noodles, uncooked
- 1 10¾-ounce can condensed cream of mushroom soup
- ¾ cup (8-ounce jar) pasteurized process cheese spread
- ¾ cup (4-ounce can) sliced mushrooms, drained
- ¼ cup chopped onion
- ¼ cup milk
- 1¾ cups (10-ounce package) frozen chopped broccoli, cooked and well drained

Cook Extra Wide Egg Noodles according to package directions; drain. Combine soup, cheese spread, mushrooms, onion and milk; blend well. Lightly toss noodles and broccoli with sauce mixture. Turn into buttered 2-quart casserole. Cover and bake at 350° 25 to 30 minutes or until hot and bubbly.

Rigatoni with Cheese and Sausage

Serves 4 to 6.

- ½ pound sweet Italian sausage
- ⅓ cup chopped onion
- 1 clove garlic, minced
- 6 tablespoons butter
- 6 tablespoons unsifted all-purpose flour
- 2 cups milk
- 1½ cups shredded sharp cheese
- 1 cup grated Parmesan cheese
- ¼ teaspoon salt
- ⅛ teaspoon pepper
- 3½ cups (8 ounces) Rigatoni, uncooked
- 2 fresh tomatoes, thinly sliced

Bake sausage at 350° 30 minutes; cool. Slice thin; set aside. Meanwhile, sauté onion and garlic in butter until tender, but not brown; blend in flour. Gradually add milk; cook, stirring constantly, over medium heat until mixture begins to boil. Remove from heat. Add 1 cup sharp cheese, Parmesan cheese, salt and pepper; blend well until cheeses are melted. Cook Rigatoni according to package directions for 12 minutes; drain. Stir Rigatoni and sausage slices into cheese sauce. Spread half the Rigatoni mixture in lightly buttered 2-quart casserole or baking dish. Layer with half the tomato slices and ¼ cup sharp cheese. Top with remaining Rigatoni mixture, sliced tomatoes and sharp cheese. Bake at 350° 35 to 40 minutes.

Cheese 'n' Greens Elbow Bake

Serves 4.

- 2 cups (8 ounces) Elbow Macaroni, uncooked
- 2 cups shredded Monterey Jack cheese
- 2 cups (16 ounces) sour cream
- 2 eggs
- 1¾ cups (10-ounce package) frozen chopped broccoli, cooked and drained
- 1 teaspoon salt
- ⅛ teaspoon pepper

Cook Elbow Macaroni according to package directions; drain. Combine 1 cup cheese, sour cream, eggs, broccoli, salt and pepper in large bowl. Stir in Elbow Macaroni. Spoon into 2-quart casserole; top with remaining 1 cup cheese. Bake at 350° 30 minutes or until hot and bubbly.

Florentine Tuna-Noodle Casserole

Serves 4.

- Basic White Sauce (recipe below)
- 6 ounces Medium Egg Noodles, uncooked
- 1¼ cups (10-ounce package) frozen chopped spinach, cooked and well drained
- 2 6½-ounce cans tuna, drained
- 2 ounces process Gruyère cheese, grated Paprika

Prepare Basic White Sauce. Cook Medium Egg Noodles according to package directions; drain. Layer noodles, spinach and tuna in buttered 2½-quart casserole. Pour white sauce on top. Sprinkle with cheese and paprika. Bake at 375° 20 minutes or until hot and bubbly.

Basic White Sauce

- ⅓ cup butter or margarine
- ½ cup chopped onion
- ⅓ cup unsifted all-purpose flour
- 1 chicken bouillon cube
- ¾ teaspoon salt
- ¼ teaspoon white pepper
- ⅛ teaspoon nutmeg
- 2 cups milk
- 1 cup water

Melt butter; sauté onion over medium heat until tender but not brown. Reduce heat; blend in flour, bouillon cube, salt, white pepper and nutmeg. Gradually add milk, then water. Cook, stirring constantly, until sauce boils; boil and stir 1 minute.

Vegetarian Dishes

Oriental Casserole

Serves 4 to 6.

  6 ounces Medium Egg Noodles, uncooked
  2 cups (6-ounce package) frozen Chinese pea pods,
    thawed and drained
  2 cups (14-ounce can) bean sprouts, drained
  1 cup (8-ounce can) sliced water chestnuts, drained
  1 cup chopped celery
  ½ cup chopped onion
  ½ cup chopped green pepper
  1 10¾-ounce can condensed cream of
    mushroom soup
  ¾ cup (4-ounce can) sliced mushrooms with liquid
  ⅔ cup milk
  3 tablespoons butter, melted
  1 tablespoon soy sauce
  ½ teaspoon pepper
  ¼ teaspoon dry mustard
  ¼ teaspoon dillweed
    Soy sauce, optional

Cook Medium Egg Noodles according to package directions; drain. Combine with remaining ingredients and place in buttered 3-quart casserole. Bake, covered, at 375° 35 minutes or until hot and bubbly. Serve with additional soy sauce, if desired.

Mostaccioli Delmonico

Serves 4.

  ½ cup chopped green pepper
  ⅓ cup finely chopped onion
  ⅓ cup finely chopped celery
  ½ clove garlic, minced
  2 tablespoons butter
  2 tablespoons olive oil
  ¼ cup chopped stuffed green olives
  ¼ cup chopped fresh parsley
  1¾ cups (15½-ounce jar) spaghetti sauce
  3 cups (8 ounces) Mostaccioli, uncooked
  ⅓ cup grated Parmesan cheese

Sauté green pepper, onion, celery and garlic in butter and oil 10 minutes or until tender, but not brown. Add olives, parsley and sauce; cover and simmer 10 minutes. Cook Mostaccioli according to package directions; drain. Toss with sauce; sprinkle with Parmesan cheese.

Cheesy Spinach-Stuffed Manicotti

Serves 6 to 8.

  1 8-ounce box Manicotti, uncooked
  1¼ cups (10-ounce package) frozen chopped spinach,
    thawed and well drained
  2 cups (8 ounces) shredded mozzarella cheese
  1 cup ricotta cheese
  1 egg
  ½ teaspoon garlic powder
  ¼ teaspoon pepper
  3½ cups (32-ounce jar) spaghetti sauce

Cook Manicotti according to package directions for 10 minutes; drain. Cool in single layer on waxed paper or aluminum foil to keep Manicotti from sticking together. Combine spinach, mozzarella and ricotta cheese, egg, garlic powder and pepper; spoon into Manicotti. Spread thin layer of sauce on bottom of 9 x 13 x 2-inch baking pan; arrange filled Manicotti in a single layer over sauce. Cover with remaining sauce. Cover with aluminum foil; bake at 375° 35 minutes or until hot and bubbly.

Cheese-Filled Jumbo Shells

Makes 36.

  1 12-ounce box Jumbo Shells, uncooked
  4 cups (2 pounds) ricotta cheese
  2 cups (8 ounces) shredded mozzarella cheese
  ¾ cup grated Parmesan cheese
  3 eggs
  1 tablespoon chopped parsley
  ¾ teaspoon oregano
  ½ teaspoon salt
  ¼ teaspoon pepper
  3½ cups (32-ounce jar) spaghetti sauce
    Grated Parmesan cheese, optional

Cook Jumbo Shells according to package directions for about 15 minutes; drain. Cool in single layer on waxed paper or aluminum foil to keep shells from sticking together. Combine cheeses, eggs, parsley, oregano, salt and pepper. Fill each shell with about 2 tablespoons cheese mixture. Spread thin layer of sauce on bottom of 9 x 13 x 2-inch baking pan. Place shells, open-side down, in single layer in pan; cover with remaining sauce. Sprinkle with additional Parmesan cheese, if desired. Cover with foil; bake at 350° about 35 minutes or until hot and bubbly.

Lasagne Roll-Ups

Makes 16 to 20.

1 pound Rippled Edge Lasagne, uncooked
4 cups (2 pounds) ricotta *or* cottage cheese
1 cup (4 ounces) shredded mozzarella cheese
1 cup chopped fresh spinach *or* ½ cup chopped fresh parsley
¼ cup grated Parmesan cheese
1 egg
¼ teaspoon salt
¼ teaspoon pepper
4 cups (32-ounce jar plus ½ cup water) spaghetti sauce
Grated Parmesan cheese, optional

Cook Lasagne according to package directions; drain well. Separate and lay flat on waxed paper or aluminum foil to keep pieces from sticking together. Combine ricotta, mozzarella, spinach, Parmesan, egg, salt and pepper for filling. Spread about ¼ cup cheese filling on each piece of La-sagne to within 1 inch of one end; beginning at filled end, roll up jelly-roll fashion. Pour about 1 cup sauce on bottom of 9 x 13 x 2-inch baking pan. Place roll-ups, seam-side down, in single layer in pan; cover with remaining sauce. Sprin-kle with additional Parmesan cheese, if desired. Cover with foil; bake at 350° 35 to 40 minutes or until filling is hot and bubbly.

Easy Manicotti with Cheese

Serves 6 to 8.

3½ cups (32-ounce jar) spaghetti sauce
1 cup water
2 cups (15-ounce container) ricotta cheese
2 cups (8 ounces) shredded mozzarella cheese
¼ cup grated Parmesan cheese
2 tablespoons chopped parsley
½ teaspoon salt
¼ teaspoon pepper
1 8-ounce box Manicotti, uncooked
Grated Parmesan cheese, optional

Heat spaghetti sauce and water in saucepan to boiling; reduce heat and keep warm. Combine cheeses, parsley, salt and pepper; spoon mixture into uncooked Manicotti. Pour 1 cup sauce on bottom of 9 x 13 x 2-inch pan; arrange filled Manicotti in a single layer over sauce. Pour re-maining sauce over Manicotti; sprinkle with ad-ditional Parmesan cheese, if desired. Cover with foil; bake at 400° 60 minutes or until hot and bubbly. Remove foil; bake 15 minutes longer.

Pasta Primavera

Serves 4.

3 cups (8 ounces) Cut Fusilli, uncooked
3 cups thinly sliced zucchini
1 cup sweet red pepper strips, cut in 1-inch pieces
1 cup green pepper strips, cut in 1-inch pieces
2 cloves garlic, minced
½ cup olive oil
Salt and pepper to taste
Grated Parmesan cheese, optional

Cook Fusilli according to package directions; drain. Meanwhile, sauté zucchini, red and green pepper and garlic in oil until vegetables are just tender. Toss hot Fusilli with sautéed vegetable mixture; season with salt and pepper. Serve with Parmesan cheese, if desired.

Vegetable Lasagne

Serves 10 to 12.

1 pound Rippled Edge Lasagne, uncooked
1¾ cups (10-ounce package) frozen chopped broccoli, cooked and well drained
1½ cups (10-ounce package) frozen peas and carrots, cooked and well drained
2 cups (15-ounce container) ricotta cheese
2 eggs
1 teaspoon garlic salt
¼ teaspoon pepper
1 11-ounce can condensed Cheddar cheese soup
1½ cups milk
2 cups (8 ounces) shredded mozzarella cheese
½ cup grated Parmesan cheese

Cook Lasagne according to package directions; drain well. Separate and lay flat on waxed paper or aluminum foil to keep pieces from sticking together. Combine vegetables, ricotta, eggs, gar-lic salt and pepper for filling. Combine soup and milk for sauce; blend until mixture is smooth. Pour a thin layer of sauce (about ¼ cup) on bot-tom of 9 x 13 x 2-inch pan. Arrange 4 pieces of Lasagne lengthwise over sauce, overlapping edges. Spread ⅓ of filling over Lasagne; sprinkle with ½ cup mozzarella and 2 tablespoons Par-mesan and cover with ½ cup sauce. Repeat lay-ers of Lasagne, filling, mozzarella, Parmesan and sauce twice. Top with a layer of Lasagne and remaining sauce; sprinkle with remaining ½ cup mozzarella and 2 tablespoons Parmesan. Cover with foil; bake at 350° 40 minutes or until hot and bubbly. Remove foil; bake an additional 10 minutes until lightly browned.

Vegetarian Dishes

Old-Fashioned Macaroni and Cheese

Serves 6 to 8.

- **4 cups (16 ounces) Elbow Macaroni, uncooked**
- **4 cups (1 pound) shredded Cheddar or American cheese**
- **2 teaspoons salt**
- **¼ teaspoon pepper**
- **⅓ cup melted butter or margarine**
- **6 cups milk**

Cook Elbow Macaroni according to package directions; drain. Arrange macaroni, cheese, salt and pepper in buttered 5-quart casserole or 9 x 13 x 2-inch pan. Pour melted butter over macaroni. Carefully pour milk into casserole at one corner. Bake, uncovered, at 350° 1 hour.

Eggplant Lasagne

Serves 6 to 8.

- **8 ounces (about 9 pieces) Rippled Edge Lasagne, uncooked**
- **3½ cups (29-ounce can) tomato puree**
- **1¾ cups (14½-ounce can) stewed tomatoes with liquid**
- **⅔ cup (6-ounce can) tomato paste**
- **1 tablespoon oregano**
- **1 teaspoon salt**
- **½ teaspoon pepper**
- **2 cups (15-ounce container) ricotta cheese**
- **1 tablespoon parsley flakes**
- **2 eggs**
- **2 tablespoons milk**
- **2 cups ⅛-inch thick eggplant slices**
- **½ cup grated Parmesan cheese**
- **2 cups (8 ounces) shredded mozzarella cheese**

Cook Lasagne according to package directions; drain. Separate and lay flat on waxed paper or aluminum foil to keep pieces from sticking together. Combine tomato puree, stewed tomatoes with liquid, tomato paste, oregano, ½ teaspoon salt and ¼ teaspoon pepper in 3-quart saucepan; heat to boiling. Reduce heat and keep warm. Combine ricotta, parsley, remaining ½ teaspoon salt and ¼ teaspoon pepper, 1 egg and milk for filling. Pour 1 cup sauce on bottom of 9 x 13 x 2-inch pan; arrange layer of Lasagne (3 pieces) over sauce. Dip eggplant slices into remaining egg which has been lightly beaten and then roll in Parmesan; arrange over Lasagne. Pour 1 cup sauce over top; sprinkle with 1 cup mozzarella. Arrange layer of Lasagne over sauce; spread cheese filling over Lasagne and cover with 1 cup sauce. Top with layer of Lasagne and remaining sauce; sprinkle with remaining 1 cup mozzarella. Cover with foil; bake at 350° 25 minutes or until hot and bubbly. Remove foil; bake about 10 minutes longer until lightly browned. Allow to stand about 10 minutes before cutting.

Spaghettini Ratatouille

Serves 8 to 10.

- **3 cups (about 1 pound) thinly sliced zucchini**
- **2 cups green pepper strips, cut in 1-inch pieces**
- **1 cup sliced onions**
- **1 clove garlic, minced**
- **1 teaspoon basil**
- **2 tablespoons olive or vegetable oil**
- **4 cups (about ¾ pound) peeled and cubed eggplant**
- **3½ cups (28-ounce can) tomatoes with liquid, chopped**
- **1 teaspoon salt**
- **¼ teaspoon pepper**
- **16 ounces Thin Spaghetti, uncooked**

Sauté zucchini, green pepper, onions, garlic and basil in oil in large skillet 5 minutes. Stir in eggplant, tomatoes with liquid, salt and pepper. Cover; cook over low heat 20 to 25 minutes, stirring occasionally. Uncover; cook 5 minutes longer. Cook Thin Spaghetti according to package directions; drain. Toss with vegetables.

Mostaccioli al Forno

Serves 4 to 6.

- **1¼ cups (10-ounce package) frozen chopped spinach**
- **2 cups (15-ounce container) ricotta cheese**
- **3 eggs, lightly beaten**
- **⅔ cup grated Parmesan cheese**
- **1 cup (4 ounces) shredded mozzarella cheese**
- **⅓ cup chopped fresh parsley**
- **1 teaspoon salt**
- **¼ teaspoon pepper**
- **3 cups (8 ounces) Mostaccioli, uncooked**
- **3½ cups (32-ounce jar) spaghetti sauce**
- **2 tablespoons grated Parmesan cheese**

Cook spinach according to package directions for 1 minute; drain. Press out excess moisture. Combine spinach, ricotta, eggs, ⅔ cup Parmesan, ⅔ cup mozzarella, parsley, salt and pepper; set aside. Cook Mostaccioli according to package directions for 10 minutes; drain. Combine Mostaccioli with 2½ cups sauce. Arrange half the Mostaccioli in bottom of 9-inch square baking dish. Layer spinach mixture evenly over Mostaccioli; cover with remaining Mostaccioli. Spread remaining sauce over top; sprinkle with ⅓ cup mozzarella and 2 tablespoons Parmesan cheese. Bake at 350° 35 to 40 minutes.

Noodle Onion Pie

Serves 6 to 8.

Cheddar Crust (recipe below)
3 ounces Medium Egg Noodles, uncooked
2 cups thinly sliced onions
2 tablespoons butter
2 eggs
1 cup milk, scalded
½ teaspoon salt
¼ teaspoon pepper
1 cup (4 ounces) shredded Cheddar cheese

Prepare Cheddar Crust; set aside. Cook Medium Egg Noodles according to package directions; drain. Meanwhile, sauté onions in butter until tender, but not brown. Remove from heat; add noodles and toss lightly. Place in unbaked crust. Beat eggs slightly; slowly stir in milk, salt, pepper and cheese. Pour mixture over noodles. Bake at 325° 30 to 35 minutes or until knife inserted in center comes out clean. Allow to stand about 10 minutes before cutting.

Cheddar Crust

1 cup (4 ounces) shredded Cheddar cheese
¾ cup unsifted all-purpose flour
½ teaspoon salt
¼ teaspoon dry mustard
¼ cup melted butter *or* margarine

Combine all ingredients in bowl; mix with pastry blender or fork until smooth. Knead about 1 minute to soften. Line a 9-inch pie plate with the cheese mixture, pressing firmly on bottom and up side, fluting around rim.

Golden Carrot Fusilli

Serves 4 to 6.

3 cups thinly sliced carrots
½ cup chopped onion
½ cup butter *or* margarine
3 cups (8 ounces) Cut Fusilli, uncooked
⅓ cup grated Parmesan cheese
¼ teaspoon salt
¼ teaspoon pepper

Sauté carrots and onion in butter until tender, but not brown. Meanwhile, cook Fusilli according to package directions; drain. Toss hot Fusilli with carrot mixture, Parmesan cheese, salt and pepper.

Broccoli-Cheese Squares

Serves 6.

1¼ cups (8 ounces) Acini di Pepe, uncooked
3 tablespoons butter
4 eggs
1 cup unsifted all-purpose flour
1 cup milk
1 teaspoon salt
1 teaspoon baking powder
4 cups (1 pound) shredded Cheddar cheese
3½ cups (2 10-ounce packages) frozen chopped broccoli, thawed and drained
2 tablespoons finely chopped onion
Seasoned salt, optional

Cook Acini di Pepe according to package directions; drain. Melt butter in 9 x 13 x 2-inch baking pan; set aside. Beat eggs in large bowl; add flour, milk, salt and baking powder and mix thoroughly. Stir in cheese, broccoli, onion and Acini di Pepe. Spread in prepared pan; sprinkle with seasoned salt, if desired. Bake at 350° 30 to 35 minutes or until knife inserted near center comes out clean. Let stand 15 minutes before cutting.

Sicilian Skillet Perciatelli

Serves 4.

8 ounces Perciatelli, uncooked
½ cup chopped onion
1 clove garlic, minced
¼ cup olive oil
2 cups (9-ounce package) frozen Italian green beans, thawed and drained
2 cups (16-ounce can) chick-peas, drained
1 teaspoon salt
¼ teaspoon pepper

Break Perciatelli in half. Cook according to package directions; drain. Meanwhile, sauté onion and garlic in oil in medium skillet until tender, but not brown. Add green beans; sauté 3 minutes. Add chick-peas, salt and pepper; sauté 1 minute. Toss hot Perciatelli with vegetables.

Side Dishes

Garden Skillet

Serves 4 to 6.

- 1 cup ¼-inch zucchini slices
- 1 cup sliced carrots
- ½ cup chopped onion
- ¼ cup butter *or* margarine
- 3 cups water
- ½ teaspoon basil
- 2¼ cups (8 ounces) Rings, uncooked
  Salt and pepper to taste

Sauté zucchini, carrots and onion in butter in 10-inch skillet until tender. Add water and basil; bring to a boil. Stir in uncooked Rings. Reduce heat to low; cover and simmer 10 minutes or until Rings are tender. Season with salt and pepper.

Easy Acini di Pepe Medley

Serves 4 to 6.

- 1 cup sliced green onions
- ½ cup chopped green pepper
- 2 tablespoons vegetable oil
- 2½ cups water
- 2 chicken bouillon cubes
- ½ teaspoon garlic salt
- 1¼ cups (8 ounces) Acini di Pepe, uncooked
- ¼ cup chopped pimiento
  Salt and pepper to taste

Sauté onions and green pepper in oil in 10-inch skillet until tender. Add water, bouillon and garlic salt; bring to a boil. Stir in uncooked Acini di Pepe. Reduce heat to low; cover and simmer 12 minutes or until Acini di Pepe is tender. Stir in pimiento, salt and pepper.

Mushroom and Bacon Skillet

Serves 4 to 6.

- ¼ pound bacon
- ½ cup chopped onion
- ½ pound fresh mushrooms, sliced
- 2 cups water
- 1 tablespoon instant chicken bouillon
- ½ teaspoon salt
- 1¼ cups (8 ounces) Orzo, uncooked
- ¼ cup chopped fresh parsley

Sauté bacon in 10-inch skillet until crisp; drain, reserving drippings. Crumble bacon; set aside. Sauté onion and mushrooms in reserved bacon drippings until tender, but not brown. Add water, bouillon, salt and uncooked Orzo. Bring to a boil

over medium heat; reduce heat to low. Cover tightly; simmer 12 minutes or until Orzo is tender. Stir in crumbled bacon and parsley.

Spaghettini Carbonara

Serves 3 to 4.

- 6 slices bacon
- ½ cup chopped onion
- ½ cup white wine
- 8 ounces Thin Spaghetti, uncooked
- 2 eggs, lightly beaten
- ¼ cup grated Parmesan cheese
- 3 tablespoons chopped fresh parsley
- ½ teaspoon salt
- ¼ teaspoon pepper

Sauté bacon until crisp; drain on paper towels, reserving drippings. Crumble bacon; set aside. Sauté onion in reserved bacon drippings until tender and lightly browned. Add crumbled bacon and wine to onion; cook over medium heat until very hot and wine is almost evaporated. Cook Thin Spaghetti according to package directions. Drain well and place in warm serving dish large enough for tossing. Add bacon mixture, eggs, cheese, parsley, salt and pepper; toss until spaghetti is well coated.

Easy Orzo Side Dish

Serves 4 to 6.

- 1 cup chopped onions
- 2 tablespoons butter *or* oil
- 1¼ cups (8 ounces) Orzo, uncooked
- 3½ cups (2 13¾- *or* 14½-ounce cans) chicken *or* beef broth *or* equivalent*

Sauté onions in butter in 10-inch skillet until tender, but not brown. Add Orzo; cook over medium heat until golden, stirring occasionally. Add broth; cook, stirring frequently, until all liquid is absorbed and Orzo is tender, about 15 to 18 minutes. Season to taste.

*For variety in flavor, use any homemade stock, canned bouillon, dry onion or mushroom-onion soup mix or bouillon cubes prepared to equal 3½ cups of liquid.

Mushroom and Bacon Skillet (top)
Garden Skillet (middle)
Easy Acini di Pepe Medley (bottom)

Rigatoni with Tomato and Basil Sauce

Serves 4 to 6.

    ¼ cup chopped onion
    1 clove garlic, minced
    ¼ cup olive oil
    3½ cups (2 14½-ounce cans) sliced stewed tomatoes
        with liquid
    6 fresh basil leaves or 1 tablespoon dried basil
    1 teaspoon salt
    3½ cups (8 ounces) Rigatoni, uncooked
        Fresh parsley, optional

Sauté onion and garlic in oil in medium skillet until onion is tender, but not brown. Add tomatoes with liquid, basil and salt; bring to boil over medium heat. Reduce heat; simmer 20 minutes, stirring occasionally. Cook Rigatoni according to package directions; drain. Toss immediately with sauce. Garnish with fresh parsley, if desired.

Cheese and Broccoli Shells

Serves 3 to 4.

    1 10-ounce package frozen broccoli spears
    2½ cups (8 ounces) Shell Macaroni, uncooked
    ¾ cup (8-ounce jar) pasteurized process cheese
        spread

Cook broccoli according to package directions; drain well and cut into small pieces. Cook Shell Macaroni according to package directions; drain well. Gently toss shells and broccoli with cheese spread until thoroughly coated.

Easy Rotini and Mushrooms

Serves 4 to 6.

    ½ cup chopped onion
    1 clove garlic, minced
    2 tablespoons butter
    1½ cups (8-ounce can) sliced mushrooms with liquid
    2 cups water
    3 beef bouillon cubes
    3 cups (8 ounces) Rotini, uncooked
    ½ cup chopped fresh parsley
        Salt and pepper to taste

Sauté onion and garlic in butter in 10-inch skillet until tender, but not brown. Add mushrooms with liquid, water and bouillon; bring to a boil. Stir in uncooked Rotini. Reduce heat to low; cover and simmer 15 minutes or until Rotini is tender. Stir in parsley, salt and pepper.

Macaroni and Cheese

Serves 6.

    2 cups (8 ounces) Elbow Macaroni, uncooked
    3 tablespoons butter
    3 tablespoons flour
    1 teaspoon salt
    1½ cups milk
    1½ cups (6 ounces) shredded process Cheddar cheese

Cook Elbow Macaroni according to package directions; drain. Meanwhile, melt butter over low heat; blend in flour and salt. Gradually add milk and 1 cup cheese. Cook over low heat, stirring constantly, until sauce is thickened and cheese melted. Add cooked macaroni; mix well. Place in buttered 2-quart casserole. Sprinkle with remaining ½ cup cheese. Bake at 375° about 20 minutes or until hot and bubbly.

Macaroni Spinach Tortine

Serves 6.

    Butter
    Fine dry bread crumbs
    1½ cups (6 ounces) Elbow Macaroni, uncooked
    4 eggs
    ¼ teaspoon garlic salt
    Dash pepper
    1 cup (8 ounces) ricotta cheese
    ½ cup grated Parmesan cheese
    1¼ cups (10-ounce package) frozen chopped spinach,
        thawed and well drained

Butter bottom and sides of 9-inch square pan; add some fine dry bread crumbs and tilt pan until coated. Cook Elbow Macaroni according to package directions; drain. Beat 3 eggs thoroughly with garlic salt and pepper in large mixing bowl; stir in cheeses. Squeeze excess water from spinach; add with macaroni to cheese mixture. Blend thoroughly. Place mixture in prepared pan; smooth surface with spatula. Beat remaining egg in small bowl; brush on top of mixture with pastry brush. Bake at 350° 25 to 30 minutes or until knife inserted in center comes out clean. Serve warm.

Note: This recipe can be prepared a day ahead and refrigerated uncut. To serve, allow to come to room temperature and heat in foil at 350° 5 to 10 minutes before cutting.

Spaghetti and Cauliflower All'Olio

Serves 4 to 6.

- **8 ounces Spaghetti, uncooked**
- **2 cloves garlic, minced**
- **¼ cup olive oil**
- **2 cups chopped cooked cauliflower** *or*
  1 10-ounce package frozen cauliflower, thawed, drained and chopped
- **1 teaspoon salt**
  Fresh parsley, optional

Cook Spaghetti according to package directions; drain. Meanwhile, sauté garlic in oil until garlic is brown. Add cauliflower and salt; sauté 2 minutes. Toss Spaghetti with cauliflower mixture; garnish with fresh parsley, if desired.

Fusilli Tomato Carbonara

Serves 6 to 8.

- **8 slices bacon**
- **¼ cup chopped onion**
- **1 clove garlic, minced**
- **3½ cups (28-ounce can) tomatoes with liquid, cut into small pieces**
- **6 fresh basil leaves,** *or* **1 tablespoon dried basil**
- **1 teaspoon salt**
- **6 cups (16 ounces) Cut Fusilli, uncooked**

Fry bacon in large skillet until crisp; drain on paper towels, reserving drippings. Crumble bacon. Stir onion and garlic into bacon drippings; cook until onion is tender, but not brown. Add tomatoes with liquid, basil and salt; bring to a boil over medium heat. Reduce heat; simmer 20 minutes, stirring occasionally. Cook Fusilli according to package directions; drain well. Add tomato mixture and bacon to Fusilli; toss lightly.

Spaghettini with Ricotta

Serves 4 to 6.

- **8 ounces Thin Spaghetti, uncooked**
- **¼ cup butter** *or* **margarine, melted**
- **1 cup ricotta cheese**
- **2 tablespoons minced fresh parsley**
  Salt and pepper to taste
  Grated Parmesan cheese

Cook Thin Spaghetti according to package directions. Drain well and place in warm serving dish large enough for tossing. Add melted butter, ricotta and parsley; toss until spaghetti is well coated. Season with salt and pepper; sprinkle with Parmesan cheese.

No-Bake Macaroni and Cheese

Serves 4 to 6.

- **2 tablespoons butter**
- **2 tablespoons flour**
- **½ teaspoon salt**
- **1 cup milk**
- **1 cup (4 ounces) shredded sharp Cheddar cheese**
- **2 cups (8 ounces) Elbow Macaroni, uncooked**
  Fresh parsley, optional

Melt butter in 2-quart saucepan; remove from heat. Add flour and salt; stir until smooth. Return to heat; gradually add milk, stirring constantly until thickened. Add cheese; stir until smooth and thick. Meanwhile, cook Elbow Macaroni according to package directions; drain. Mix macaroni with cheese sauce until well coated. Garnish with parsley, if desired.

Fettuccini Alfredo

Serves 4 to 6.

- **1 12-ounce box Fettuccini, uncooked**
- **½ cup butter** *or* **margarine, softened**
- **½ cup heavy** *or* **whipping cream at room temperature**
- **¾ cup grated Parmesan cheese**
- **2 tablespoons snipped parsley**
  Salt and pepper to taste

Cook Fettuccini according to package directions. Drain well and place in warm serving dish large enough for tossing. Add butter, cream, cheese and parsley; toss until Fettuccini is well coated. Season with salt and pepper.

Fettuccini Carbonara

Serves 4 to 6.

- **¼ pound bacon**
- **1 12-ounce box Fettuccini, uncooked**
- **¼ cup butter** *or* **margarine, softened**
- **½ cup heavy** *or* **whipping cream at room temperature**
- **½ cup grated Parmesan cheese**
- **2 eggs, lightly beaten**
- **2 tablespoons snipped parsley**

Sauté bacon until crisp; drain well and crumble. Cook Fettuccini according to package directions. Drain well and place in warm serving dish large enough for tossing. Add crumbled bacon, butter, cream, cheese, eggs and parsley; toss until Fettuccini is well coated.

Sauces

Basic Tomato Sauce

Makes enough sauce for 8 ounces of pasta.

- ½ cup chopped onion
- 1 clove garlic, minced
- ¼ cup olive or vegetable oil
- 3½ cups (28-ounce can) crushed tomatoes or tomato puree
- 1 tablespoon chopped parsley
- 2 teaspoons sugar
- 2 teaspoons basil
- ½ teaspoon oregano
- ½ teaspoon salt
- ¼ teaspoon pepper

Sauté onion and garlic in oil in 2-quart saucepan until tender, but not brown. Stir in remaining ingredients; simmer 15 to 20 minutes, stirring occasionally.

Cheese Pasta Sauce

Makes enough sauce for 8 ounces of pasta.

- ½ pound mild Italian sausage, casing removed
- ½ cup chopped onion
- ½ cup chopped carrots
- ¾ cup (4-ounce can) sliced mushrooms, drained
- 1 clove garlic, minced
- 1¾ cups (15-ounce can) tomato sauce
- 1 cup water
- 1 teaspoon Italian seasoning
- 1 cup (4 ounces) shredded Cheddar cheese
- 1 cup (4 ounces) shredded Provolone cheese

Cook sausage, onion, carrots, mushrooms and garlic in large skillet until carrots are tender, about 10 minutes; drain off excess drippings. Add tomato sauce, water and Italian seasoning; simmer, uncovered, 15 minutes. Stir in cheeses until melted.

Herb and Butter Sauce

Makes enough sauce for 8 ounces of pasta.

- ½ cup butter
- 2 tablespoons chopped fresh parsley
- 1 tablespoon chopped chives
- ½ teaspoon garlic salt

Melt butter in small saucepan. Stir in parsley, chives and garlic salt.

Garlic and Oil Sauce

Makes enough sauce for 8 ounces of pasta.

- 2 cloves garlic, minced
- ¼ cup olive oil
- 1 teaspoon salt
- ¼ cup chopped fresh parsley

Sauté garlic in oil until garlic is brown. Stir in salt and parsley.

Basic Meat Sauce

Makes enough sauce for 1 pound of pasta.

- 1 pound ground beef or pork
- ½ cup chopped onion
- 1 clove garlic, minced
- 3½ cups (28-ounce can) tomato puree or crushed tomatoes
- ⅔ cup (6-ounce can) tomato paste
- 2 cups water
- 1 tablespoon chopped parsley
- 1 tablespoon sugar
- 2 teaspoons basil
- 1 teaspoon salt
- ⅛ teaspoon pepper

Sauté ground beef in large skillet until brown. Add onion and garlic; cook until onion is tender. Stir in remaining ingredients; simmer 30 minutes.

Easy Meat Sauce

Makes enough sauce for 8 ounces of pasta.

- 1 pound ground beef
- ½ cup chopped onion
- ¼ cup chopped green pepper
- 2 cups (2 8-ounce cans) tomato sauce
- 1 teaspoon sugar
- 1 teaspoon salt
- ½ teaspoon oregano
- ½ teaspoon thyme
- ¼ teaspoon pepper
- ¼ teaspoon basil

Brown ground beef, onion and green pepper in 3-quart saucepan until onion is tender. Stir in remaining ingredients. Cover; simmer 25 to 30 minutes, stirring occasionally.

Herb and Butter Sauce (top)
Basic Tomato Sauce (bottom)

Sauces

Money-Saver Meat Sauce

Makes enough sauce for 8 ounces of pasta.

- ¾ pound ground beef
- ¼ cup sliced onion
- 1 clove garlic, finely chopped
- 1½ teaspoons vegetable oil
- 1¾ cups (14½-ounce can) tomatoes with liquid
- 1 cup (8-ounce can) tomato sauce
- 1 teaspoon salt
- ¼ teaspoon oregano
- ⅛ teaspoon pepper

Brown ground beef, onion and garlic in oil in large skillet. Add remaining ingredients; cook 15 minutes, stirring occasionally.

Creamy Vegetable Cheese Sauce

Makes enough sauce for 8 ounces of pasta.

- ½ cup butter *or* margarine
- 1 cup milk
- ¼ cup white wine
- ½ teaspoon white pepper
- ½ teaspoon salt
- ¼ teaspoon nutmeg
- 1 pound process American cheese, cubed
- 1¾ cups (10-ounce package) frozen chopped broccoli, thawed and well drained
- 1½ cups (10-ounce package) frozen peas and carrots, thawed and well drained
- 2 cups (10-ounce package) frozen cauliflower, thawed and well drained

Melt butter in 3-quart saucepan; stir in milk, wine and spices. Add cheese; cook over medium heat, stirring constantly, until cheese is melted and mixture is smooth. Add vegetables; simmer 15 minutes, stirring occasionally.

Tuna Sauce

Makes enough sauce for 8 ounces of pasta.

- 1 clove garlic, minced
- ⅓ cup chopped onion
- 2 tablespoons vegetable oil
- 3½ cups (28-ounce can) tomatoes, crushed
- 1 tablespoon chopped fresh parsley
- 2 teaspoons sugar
- ½ teaspoon basil
- ½ teaspoon oregano
- 1 6½-ounce can tuna, drained and flaked

Sauté garlic and onion in oil in 3-quart saucepan until onion is tender, but not brown. Add tomatoes, parsley, sugar, basil and oregano; cook, uncovered, about 20 minutes or until sauce thickens. Stir in tuna; heat thoroughly.

Herb Meat Sauce

Makes enough sauce for 8 ounces of pasta.

- 1 pound ground beef
- 2 cups crushed tomatoes
- 1 cup (8-ounce can) tomato sauce
- 1 teaspoon sugar
- 1 teaspoon seasoned salt
- ¼ teaspoon oregano
- ¼ teaspoon basil
- ¼ teaspoon garlic powder

Brown ground beef in large skillet; drain off excess drippings. Reduce heat; stir in remaining ingredients. Cover and simmer 20 to 25 minutes, stirring frequently.

Meat Sauce

Makes enough sauce for 8 ounces of pasta.

- ⅓ cup chopped onion
- ¼ cup chopped carrots
- ¼ cup chopped celery
- 2 tablespoons butter
- 2 tablespoons vegetable oil
- ⅛ teaspoon rosemary
- ⅛ teaspoon pepper
  Dash sage
- 2 bay leaves
- ¾ pound beef round steak, cut into 1-inch cubes
- 2 cups (16-ounce can) tomatoes, crushed
- ½ teaspoon salt

Sauté onion, carrots and celery in butter and oil until tender. Add seasonings and beef cubes; cook until meat is browned. Add tomatoes and salt; simmer until meat is tender, about 30 minutes.

Quick Spaghetti Sauce and Meatballs

Makes enough sauce for 8 ounces of pasta.

- ½ pound ground beef
- ½ pound ground pork
- ½ cup flavored bread crumbs
- 1 egg, beaten
- 1 teaspoon garlic salt
- ⅛ teaspoon pepper
- ¼ cup vegetable oil
- 3½ cups (32-ounce jar) spaghetti sauce

Combine beef, pork, bread crumbs, egg, garlic salt and pepper; shape into small balls. Brown meatballs in oil in skillet; drain off excess drippings. Add sauce; simmer 10 to 15 minutes.

Note: For a thinner sauce, add 1 cup water to sauce.

Sausage Sauce

Makes enough for 1 pound of pasta.

- **1 pound hot Italian sausage, cut in 1-inch slices**
- **1 pound sweet Italian sausage, cut in 1-inch slices**
- **1½ cups water**
- **1 cup diced green pepper**
- **½ cup chopped onion**
- **3 cups (3 8-ounce cans) tomato sauce**
- **⅔ cup (6-ounce can) tomato paste**
- **Salt and pepper to taste**

Simmer sausages in ½ cup water in 3-quart covered saucepan 10 minutes. Uncover; simmer until juices cook down and sausage is browned, stirring occasionally. Remove sausage with a slotted spoon; set aside. Discard all but 1 tablespoon drippings. Sauté green pepper and onion in drippings until tender, but not brown. Add tomato sauce, tomato paste, remaining 1 cup water and salt and pepper. Add sausage; simmer, covered, 30 minutes, stirring occasionally.

Cheese Sauce

Makes enough sauce for 8 ounces of pasta.

- **2 tablespoons butter**
- **2 tablespoons flour**
- **½ teaspoon salt**
- **1 cup milk**
- **4 ounces pasteurized process cheese, cubed**

Melt butter in 2-quart saucepan; remove from heat. Add flour and salt; stir until smooth. Return to heat; gradually add milk, stirring constantly until thickened. Add process cheese; stir until smooth and thick.

Mushroom Sauce

Makes enough sauce for 8 ounces of pasta.

- **½ cup chopped onion**
- **¼ cup chopped green pepper**
- **1 clove garlic, minced**
- **¼ cup olive or vegetable oil**
- **1½ cups (8-ounce can) sliced mushrooms, drained**
- **3½ cups (29-ounce can) tomato sauce**
- **½ teaspoon oregano**
- **½ teaspoon thyme**
- **½ teaspoon basil**
- **½ teaspoon salt**
- **¼ teaspoon pepper**

Sauté onion, green pepper and garlic in oil in 3-quart saucepan until tender, but not brown. Add mushrooms; sauté 1 minute. Stir in tomato sauce and seasonings; simmer 15 to 20 minutes, stirring occasionally.

Red Clam Sauce

Makes enough sauce for 8 ounces of pasta.

- **½ cup chopped onion**
- **1 tablespoon olive oil or butter**
- **1 6½-ounce can minced clams, drained (reserve liquid)**
- **1¾ cups (15½-ounce jar) spaghetti sauce**
- **1 teaspoon parsley flakes**
- **½ teaspoon thyme**
- **¼ teaspoon basil**
- **¼ teaspoon salt**
- **⅛ teaspoon pepper**

Sauté onion in oil in 2-quart saucepan until tender, but not brown. Add clams, ¼ cup clam liquid, sauce and seasonings; simmer 15 minutes, stirring occasionally, to blend flavors.

Olive Sauce

Makes enough sauce for 8 ounces of pasta.

- **¼ cup olive oil**
- **2 cloves garlic, minced**
- **1½ cups pitted ripe olives, cut into small pieces**
- **½ cup chopped fresh parsley**
- **Salt and pepper to taste**

Heat oil in small saucepan; add garlic, but do not brown. Add olives and parsley; sauté 2 to 3 minutes or until olives are heated. Immediately toss with hot pasta of your choice. Season with salt and pepper.

Pesto Sauce

Makes enough sauce for 12 ounces of pasta.

- **4 cups cleaned fresh spinach**
- **1 cup fresh parsley**
- **¾ cup grated Parmesan cheese**
- **½ cup walnuts**
- **½ cup olive oil**
- **1 clove garlic**
- **½ teaspoon salt**
- **¼ teaspoon pepper**

Combine all ingredients in food processor or blender container. Process or blend until mixture is smooth. Immediately toss with hot pasta of your choice.

White Clam Sauce

Makes enough sauce for 8 ounces of pasta.

  4 cloves garlic, crushed
  ½ cup olive oil
  1 tablespoon flour
  4 cups (4 7½-ounce cans) chopped clams
    with liquid
1½ cups chopped fresh parsley
  ½ teaspoon salt
  ¼ teaspoon pepper

Sauté garlic in oil in medium saucepan until golden; blend in flour. Gradually stir in remaining ingredients. Cook over medium-low heat, stirring constantly, until sauce is thickened.

Spicy Barbecue Shrimp Sauce

Makes enough sauce for 8 ounces of pasta.

  ½ cup chopped onion
  ½ cup chopped celery
  ½ cup chopped green pepper
1½ cups (8-ounce package) frozen shrimp, thawed,
    peeled and deveined
  2 tablespoons vegetable oil
  1 cup (8-ounce can) tomato sauce
  ½ cup (4 ounces) bottled barbecue sauce
  ½ cup picante sauce
    Salt and pepper to taste

Sauté onion, celery, green pepper and shrimp in oil in 2-quart saucepan until tender, but not brown. Add tomato sauce, barbecue sauce and picante sauce; stir to blend. Simmer, uncovered, about 10 minutes to blend flavors. Season with salt and pepper.

Seafood Sauce

Makes enough sauce for 8 ounces of pasta.

  ¼ cup butter *or* margarine
  ¼ cup unsifted all-purpose flour
  ½ teaspoon salt
  ¼ teaspoon pepper
  2 cups milk
  2 egg yolks, beaten
  1 tablespoon sherry
  2 cups shredded cooked lobster, tuna, shrimp
    and/or crab meat

Melt butter in 3-quart saucepan; blend in flour and seasonings. Gradually add milk; cook, stirring constantly, until thickened. Add small amount of sauce to egg yolks; blend well. Return egg mixture to sauce in pan; stir until smooth. Stir in sherry and seafood; heat to serving temperature, but *do not boil.*

Chili Sauce

Makes enough sauce for 8 ounces of pasta.

  1 pound ground lean beef
  1 cup sliced onions
  1 clove garlic, minced
  2 beef bouillon cubes dissolved in
    1¾ cups boiling water
  1 tablespoon chili powder
  ½ teaspoon salt
  2 tablespoons Worcestershire sauce
  1 cup diced green pepper
  3 tablespoons flour combined with
    ¼ cup water
1¾ cups (14½-ounce can) tomatoes with liquid,
    chopped

Brown beef in large skillet. Add onions and garlic; cook and stir until onions are tender. Add bouillon, chili powder, salt, Worcestershire and green pepper. Cover and simmer 5 minutes. Gradually stir in flour mixture. Cook, stirring constantly, until sauce thickens. Add tomatoes with liquid; simmer 10 minutes.

Spaghetti Sauce with Meatballs

Makes enough for 1 pound of pasta.

    Meatballs (recipe below)
  ¼ cup vegetable oil
  ½ cup chopped onion
  1 clove garlic, minced
3½ cups (29-ounce can) tomato puree
  1 cup water
  ⅔ cup (6-ounce can) tomato paste
  1 teaspoon salt
  ½ teaspoon oregano
  ½ teaspoon basil
  ⅛ teaspoon pepper

Prepare Meatballs; brown in oil in large skillet. Drain excess drippings. Add onion and garlic; sauté 2 to 3 minutes. Add remaining ingredients; simmer 15 to 20 minutes.

Meatballs

  1 pound ground beef
  ½ pound ground pork
  ⅓ cup flavored bread crumbs
  ⅓ cup grated Parmesan cheese
  2 eggs
  1 tablespoon chopped parsley
1½ teaspoons garlic salt
  ¼ teaspoon pepper

Combine all ingredients in large bowl. Shape into small balls.

Spicy Barbecue Shrimp Sauce (top)
White Clam Sauce (bottom)

Desserts

Alphabet Dessert

Serves 6 to 8.

- 1 6-ounce package any fruit-flavored gelatin
- 2 cups boiling water
- 1 8-ounce can pineapple chunks or crushed pineapple with liquid
  Cold water
- ¾ cup Alphabets, uncooked
- 10 maraschino cherries, cut into quarters
  Whipped topping, optional

Add boiling water to gelatin in medium-size bowl; stir until dissolved. Drain pineapple, reserving liquid. Add cold water, if necessary, to pineapple liquid to make ¾ cup; stir into gelatin. Chill until partially set. Cook Alphabets according to package directions without salt; drain. Rinse with cold water to cool quickly; drain well. Fold pineapple, Alphabets and cherries into gelatin; pour into 9 x 13 x 2-inch pan. Chill until firm. Spoon into serving dishes; garnish with whipped topping, if desired.

Pasta Pudding

Serves 4 to 6.

- ⅓ cup sugar
- 2 tablespoons cornstarch
- ⅛ teaspoon salt
- 2 cups milk
- 2 egg yolks, slightly beaten
- 2 tablespoons butter
- 2 teaspoons vanilla
- ⅛ teaspoon cinnamon
- 1 cup Acini di Pepe, uncooked
- ½ cup raisins, optional
  Whipped topping and maraschino cherries, optional

Blend sugar, cornstarch and salt in 2-quart saucepan. Combine milk and egg yolks; gradually stir into sugar mixture. Cook over medium heat, stirring constantly, until mixture thickens and comes to a boil. Boil and stir 1 minute. Remove from heat; add butter, vanilla and cinnamon. Cook Acini di Pepe according to package directions without salt; drain well. Stir into pudding. Add raisins, if desired. Spoon into serving dishes. Garnish with whipped topping and cherries, if desired. Serve warm.

Lemon Noodle Pudding

Serves 6.

- 8 ounces Medium Egg Noodles, uncooked
- 3 eggs
- 1 cup small-curd cottage cheese
- ½ cup sour cream
- 4 tablespoons butter or margarine, melted
- ½ cup sugar
- 1 teaspoon cinnamon
- ½ teaspoon grated lemon peel
- ¼ teaspoon salt
- ⅛ teaspoon nutmeg
- 1 teaspoon lemon juice
- 1 teaspoon vanilla
- ¼ cup raisins, optional
- 1 cup soft bread crumbs
- ⅓ cup chopped nuts
  Light cream, optional

Cook Medium Egg Noodles according to package directions without salt; drain well. Beat eggs in medium-size bowl; stir in cottage cheese, sour cream, 2 tablespoons melted butter, sugar, cinnamon, lemon peel, salt, nutmeg, lemon juice, vanilla and raisins, if desired. Fold in cooked noodles. Pour mixture into buttered 8-inch square baking pan. Sauté bread crumbs and nuts in remaining 2 tablespoons melted butter in skillet over medium heat, stirring occasionally, until crumbs are golden. Sprinkle over top of noodle mixture. Cover and bake at 375° 25 minutes; uncover and bake 10 minutes longer. Serve warm with light cream, if desired.

Peaches 'n' Pudding

Serves 6 to 8.

- 1 cup (4 ounces) Rings, uncooked
- 1 3¾-ounce package instant vanilla pudding and pie filling
- 1 cup cold milk
- 1 cup frozen nondairy whipped topping, thawed
- 1 16-ounce can sliced peaches, drained

Cook Rings according to package directions without salt; drain. Rinse with cold water to cool quickly; drain well. Prepare pudding according to package directions using 1 cup cold milk. Fold in Rings and whipped topping. Cut peaches into bite-size pieces. Alternately layer pudding mixture and peaches in parfait glasses. Chill.

Apple Lasagne

Serves 9.

  8 ounces (about 9 pieces) Rippled Edge Lasagne,
    uncooked
  1 cup sour cream
  ¼ cup packed light brown sugar
  ⅛ teaspoon cinnamon
  1 21-ounce can apple pie filling
  ½ cup apple juice
  ¾ cup unsifted all-purpose flour
  ¼ cup plus 2 tablespoons packed light brown sugar
  6 tablespoons firm butter *or* margarine

Cook Lasagne according to package directions without salt; drain well. Separate and lay flat on waxed paper or aluminum foil to keep pieces from sticking together. Combine sour cream, ¼ cup brown sugar and cinnamon; set aside. Place 3 pieces of Lasagne on bottom of buttered 9-inch square baking pan, cutting Lasagne to fit pan if necessary; spread ⅓ pie filling over Lasagne. Spoon ½ of sour cream mixture evenly over filling; top with 3 pieces of Lasagne. Pour ¼ cup apple juice over Lasagne. Repeat layers of pie filling, sour cream mixture and Lasagne. Spread remaining pie filling over Lasagne; top with remaining ¼ cup apple juice. Combine flour and ¼ cup plus 2 tablespoons brown sugar; cut in butter until crumbly. Sprinkle mixture over Lasagne. Bake, covered, at 375° 30 minutes. Uncover; bake an additional 10 minutes. Allow to stand 15 minutes before serving. Cut into squares.

Ambrosia

Serves 6 to 8.

  1 cup Rings *or* Orzo, uncooked
  2 cups (16 ounces) sour cream
  2 cups miniature marshmallows
  2 cups flaked coconut
  2 cups (20-ounce can) pineapple chunks,
    well drained
  1 cup (11-ounce can) mandarin oranges,
    well drained

Cook Rings according to package directions; drain. Rinse with cold water to cool quickly; drain well. Combine all ingredients in large bowl; blend well. Chill.

Hawaiian Shells

Serves 4 to 6.

  1 cup Shell Macaroni *or* Ditalini, uncooked
  3 oranges, peeled and sectioned
  2 bananas, sliced
  ¾ cup flaked coconut
  1 cup pineapple yogurt

Cook Shell Macaroni according to package directions; drain. Rinse with cold water to cool quickly; drain well. Combine all ingredients in medium bowl; blend well. Chill.

Fruit-Stuffed Shells

Serves 8 to 10.

  6 ounces Jumbo Shells, uncooked
  2 cups (22-ounce can) fruit pie filling of your choice
    Confectioners' sugar

Cook Jumbo Shells according to package directions; drain well. Dry on paper towels. Fry shells, a few at a time, in deep oil in deep-fat fryer or frypan at 375° about 2 minutes or until lightly browned. Stir to separate. Drain on paper towels. Fill each shell with about 2 tablespoons pie filling; sprinkle with confectioners' sugar.

Pineapple-Apricot Kugel with Noodles

Serves 12.

    8 ounces dried apricots, chopped
    1 cup boiling water
    6 ounces Wide Egg Noodles, uncooked
    6 eggs
  1¼ cups sugar
    2 cups (16 ounces) sour cream
    2 8-ounce cans crushed pineapple, drained
    2 teaspoons lemon juice
   ½ teaspoon salt
    1 cup chopped nuts

Soak apricots in boiling water 15 minutes to soften; drain well. Cook Wide Egg Noodles according to package directions; drain. Beat eggs and sugar in large bowl 4 minutes or until thick and pale yellow; add sour cream and beat on low speed until smooth. Stir in apricots, pineapple, noodles, lemon juice and salt. Pour into buttered 9 x 13 x 2-inch baking pan; top with nuts. Bake at 350° 30 to 35 minutes. Serve warm.

Fruit and Shells Refresher

Serves 6 to 8.

- 1 cup Shell Macaroni, uncooked
- 1 cup grape halves, seeded
- 1 cup (11-ounce can) mandarin oranges, drained
- ¾ cup (8-ounce can) pineapple chunks with liquid
- 1 cup vanilla yogurt
- 1 tablespoon honey
- ½ cup broken walnuts

Cook Shell Macaroni according to package directions. Rinse with cold water to cool quickly; drain well. Combine grapes and oranges in medium-size bowl. Drain pineapple chunks, reserving 2 tablespoons juice; add pineapple chunks to fruit mixture. Combine yogurt, honey and reserved pineapple juice in small bowl; blend well. Pour dressing over fruit; toss. Add Shell Macaroni; mix well. Chill; stir in walnuts just before serving.

Pasta Fruit Medley

Serves 4 to 6.

- 1 cup Ditalini, uncooked
- ⅓ cup vegetable oil
- 3 tablespoons orange juice
- 1 teaspoon sugar
- ⅛ teaspoon salt
- 1½ cups (16-ounce can) sliced peaches, drained
- 1½ cups (16-ounce can) sliced pears, drained
- 2 cups (2 whole) fresh oranges, pared and cut in pieces
- ½ cup toasted coconut
- ¼ cup sliced almonds
  Strawberry slices, optional

Cook Ditalini according to package directions. Rinse with cold water to cool quickly; drain well. Combine oil, orange juice, sugar and salt in screw-top jar or small bowl; shake or whip with wire whisk until well blended and of a thick and creamy consistency. Combine Ditalini, peaches, pears and oranges in medium-size bowl. Pour dressing over fruit and pasta; toss lightly. Add coconut and sliced almonds; toss again. Garnish with strawberry slices, if desired.

Apple Noodle Dessert

Serves 6.

- 6 ounces Medium Egg Noodles, uncooked
- ¼ cup butter or margarine, melted
- 3½ cups (35-ounce jar) applesauce
- 2 eggs
- ¾ cup brown sugar
- 1 teaspoon vanilla
- ¾ teaspoon cinnamon
- ¼ teaspoon salt
- 1 cup raisins
- 1 cup chopped almonds
  Nondairy whipped topping

Cook Medium Egg Noodles according to package directions; drain. Toss with melted butter. Combine remaining ingredients except whipped topping; fold into noodles. Pour into a buttered 9-inch square pan; cover with aluminum foil. Bake at 375° 45 minutes. Serve warm with whipped topping.

Creamy Noodle Pudding

Serves 6.

- 4 ounces Medium Egg Noodles, uncooked
- 2 cups scalded milk
- 2 eggs, beaten
- ½ cup sugar
- ½ teaspoon salt
- 1 teaspoon vanilla
- 1 teaspoon grated lemon rind
- ½ cup seedless raisins
  Nutmeg
  Light cream, optional

Cook Medium Egg Noodles according to package directions; drain. Combine milk, eggs, sugar, salt, vanilla and lemon rind; fold in raisins and noodles. Pour into 6 buttered individual custard cups; sprinkle with nutmeg. Set custard cups in pan of hot water. Bake at 350° 1 hour. Unmold into sauce dishes. Serve warm with light cream, if desired.

Index

B
C
D
E
F
G
H
I
J
K
L

4
5
6
7
8
9
0
1